This is the true story of three girls,
typical Londoners, working,
obsessing about life, love and food.
This is also what we like to call...

The Soup Diaries

Life, Love and Soup in London

*Love
Lucy*

Lucy Mason Jensen

Copyright © 2023 by Lucy Mason Jensen
All rights reserved.

Starters

**This is the true story of three girls, typical Londoners, working, obsessing about life, love, food …
This is also what we like to call 'The Soup Diaries'**

These twenty-somethings had been friends forever; so, there was nothing off subject, as you will see in their banter. They were also new London flat owners, where they would cook, eat, drink and plan their men-chasing antics in each other's homes. Lots of soups, hangovers, cheese, chocolate and laughter.

It was also the beginning of an exciting new era – the Internet had arrived – so 'The Soup Diaries' have evolved as a period piece stemming from these emails, that were amazingly preserved, between late 1999 to the Spring of 2000.

My sister (Natalie in the book) had kept the collection, hoping that someone in their group would write it up and give them all a laugh. I eventually stole it away, after she passed, to make sister's sometime 'dream' a reality. She had always wanted this life extract published, but even more, in true sister style, she wanted the movie made. She had selected the names of the stars who would play each of them and I give the characters in this book their movie star names for several reasons – but, mostly, to protect the innocent. (Insert LOL, as they learn in the script, is more than just lots of love!)

If any of these actual stars read and approve of the manuscript, have your people call me. The actual movie would be great fun.

Love always - Big Sis/Lu

Lucy Jensen

Foreword

The Soup Diaries came about when we were mobile phoneless and people still got out of their seats to talk to colleagues working in the same room. Email was newly accessible and while there was still walking between houses and making arrangements to meet up over the landline and sticking to them, email presented an exciting way to communicate for free outside of the usual. It seemed amazing to be able to write letters to each other and have them received immediately. And may account for the length and detail involved!

Friendship groups like this one are unremarkable. There are groups of young women like us everywhere - always have been, always will be. And is our time any different? Everyone's time is special, but, looking back, the remarkable stuff was taken for granted at the time. '90s London is now a land that time forgot, with communication and socials very much IRL.

The twenties are tough. You want to claim your life and independence, but also there is little to go on at that age and ideas about how to live and what you'd like to do with the world are generally pretty sketchy - the future is still a ghostly 'up ahead'!

And now, looking back on life nearly 30 years ago, the experience is similarly misty, as there are the bare outlines of our lives in there. Mostly coming through the pages is the friendship - vibrant, energetic, lusty and reflecting a firm grip on the day to day of living. But it's hard to know now that one of us wouldn't make it to 50.

Just to add in for geography, it was possible for people in their twenties with averagely good jobs to get onto the property ladder and take a chance with less popular corners of London. Everyone in this group managed it by the age of 30 with low interest rates and a modest amount of parental backing. That seems beyond reach for most young people today. It was a special time, being young, living within 5 minutes' walk of each other, in a London that was a sparkling place to be, and beginning to grab opportunities and see where life would lead. Hope you enjoy the peek into its world and find something of your own in there too.

Cate B
(Aka LuLo)

The Soup Diaries

November 1999

November 8, 1999
From: Nat
To: Andi, Nic
Subj: Testing, testing 1, 2, 3

Girls, am I really here? Can it be so simple, do I now have complete lift off? I'm so far behind the two of you it's not true – I don't know what LOL stands for – all bloody acronyms to me – will need lots of support from you two cool birds to get up to speed. Please send replies, having computer and email is just another form of disappointment. We've all got Call Minder, just to reassure us that no one has called and now we have email to add to the list!
Oh well, ever the optimist XXX
So, what's on the menu tonight?

November 8, 1999
From: Andi
To: Nat
Subject: Testing, testing, 123 ...

Nat, thank god you're finally here. CU tonight! (First lesson in abbreviations) Don't know ... what do you think? Fancy hearty soup!

November 8, 1999
From: Nic
To: Natalie
Re: testing, testing, 123 ....

Hello sweetie!
So now you know how I spend my working day – checking mail, sending mail, jokes, pics – you name it! Anything to avoid real work! This is the perfect non-work activity, and it really helps the entire working population get through the day until they can meet up with the people who they've been emailing all day – then the following day, they all send each other mail about last night!
Get the picture- so CU tonight – I'm already looking forward to tomorrow's mail, about tonight – understand? LOL xx
I think hearty soup – ministronie – god, how do you spell it?

November 8, 1999
From: pimet@superonline.com (Ali)
To: Natalie

I'm soo happy to meet you in the oyster. This was the best of decisions for you in nowadays, believe me. I know what a feeling of freedom it is for you. Now you must load ICQ on your computer and find me there as 'le bon coeur' … this will be so funny to chat with you. Missing you. It works, yeah!

November 9, 1999
From: Natalie
To: Nic
Subj: Good morning

Dearest Nicole,
Was thinking bout you and work today when I got home at 5.30. Have actually done some work though on Pc tonight and avoided the chat rooms because you can easily lose hours that way.

Have spoken to Sue tonight and she is going to come and stay on the 19th and 20th. I know you are away one night, but can you make a session? I feel a bottle of Turkish brandy coming on and know that you would appreciate it.
Anyway, this is really meant to be a good morning call, hope you have a good day at work and thanks for condom jokes. I particularly like the Nike one. For now, that's all.
Love,
Nat

November 9, 1999
From: Nat
To: Andi
Subj: About email before breakfast

Dearest McD,

I woke up this morning (da na na na na) and I checked my email to find that I had some. It's totally fab to have lovely messages waiting for you when you first crawl out of bed. Had fab and very long message from Flo and, of course, from Ali, not so good English, but he's a proper techno geek because he is banging on about something to do with ICQ so that we can chat, do you have a clue what he's talking about? I think this will be tonight's techno challenge. For now, must really drag myself away and go to work.

Love,

Nat

November 9, 1999
From: Nat
To: Nic, Andi
Subj: Soup!

Andi, soup was just what doc ordered – despite the bottles. Think 'Hearty Ministrony' (prefer this spelling) has scared off almighty hangover until tonight. Thanks, girls, for techy lesson – you really are a couple of geeks. So pleased to know you!

What the hell, I now understand the real use of email – flirting! What a fab night, sorry the soup wasn't better, smoked mussel was really going a bit too far. I promise never again. The really sad thing is that I still wouldn't actually want to shag any of the blokes we met last night in the chat rooms, and that was them at their best. Let's face it, if you can't make yourself attractive over the ether, you have absolutely no chance in real life.

What about that saddo (not as in sado, that was the other one). I giggled about that long past my bedtime. Thank god we found the foodies room – don't think I impressed anyone with my mussel soup recipe, but certainly scored high on originality and flair with canned foods! Nic scores especially high though – very impressive behaviour – want an update later.

November 9, 1999
From: Andi
To: Natalie

What a giggle last night was ... the whole thing seems very surreal what with you having an alias of "Naomi" and talking about where serves a great eggs benedict. Oh well, it all seems like harmless fun. Hope you have a good day and I'll send you a couple of things to make you chuckle.
TTFN,
Andi

November 9, 1999
From: Natalie
To: Andi

What the frig is TTFN? Now you're just showing off!

November 9, 1999
From: Andi
To: Natalie

Heavy message from your lover!

November 9, 1999
From: Natalie
To: Andi

Dearest McD,

After having 6 hours of hard time with CAD on my desktop, I received your alien. It was a real shock for me rather than a contrast to find it singing here on the same screen – I watched several times and have been doubled up with laughter. Unfortunately, I cannot frequent musical centers anymore – time is problem, timing is another problem. I do not think that it is a shame, but maybe an unnecessary touchiness and sensitivity. I'm not sure about approving the necessity of respecting someone's exaggerated personal problem with such a self-sacrifice. Anyway, the earth is round, and it is ours.

Take care you too.

Meanwhile, I cannot send email to Nic, something is wrong with our servers, please tell her.

November 9, 1999
From: Nic
To: Natalie
Subject: email before breakfast

Hello sweetie! What time exactly did you wake up in order to check your email? You will have to give up sleeping altogether, then night sessions online can blend seamlessly in to checking your mail before breakfast. Now who's the saddo?

Anyway, call yourself a friend. I can't believe you and Andi let me do it. It's one thing to flirt, it's another totally to actually agree to meet. Let's face it, he doesn't have my number, has no idea that my real name isn't really Esmeralda and that I'm not a fashion buyer for Liberty. The reality is, of course, far more gorgeous and exotic. C'est moi, bloody lovely – okay better stop this ego masturbation and get on with this work thang. XX

Where, when and, more importantly, what is dins tonight? Nic, it could be your turn? Not sure, however, you can better the mini 2 nights in a row. Think you should bunk off work early in order to make us proper dins – I'm starving on this soup diet?

**November 10, 1999
From: Natalie
To: Nic, Andi
Subj: Night and a bottle of wine?**

Dearest both,
My tooth fairy has been during the night and now have some idea of what ICQ is. Ali has given me supposedly easy instructions to follow, but you know me. Anyone fancy coming round tonight to help with setting it up? Let me know girls. Love and kisses XXX

**November 10, 1999
From: Nic
To: Nat, Andi**

Sweeties, I think it'll be a late one tonight. Just occasionally the bank pulls out the stops and actually makes me do some work. It looks like tonight may just be one of those. Will call when I get home, if it's not too late XX

**November 10, 1999
From: Andi
To: Nic, Nat**

I'd love to see you battle through Ali's instructions, but I'm out with Kate (from Orient Express) - thought we'd do Pitcher & Piano & Thai Pot. Sorry! Nic, I miss you in the mornings - boo hoo- what about Friday as I'm off tomorrow? Nat, are you waking up each morning to a message from the tooth fairy? How lovely if you are. See ya. Big snog.
McD X

November 10, 1999
From: Natalie
To: Nic
Subj: I know the real purpose of email

The only reason why people have email at home is so that they never have to face up to the reality of work. Every time I sit down to work, I get itchy fingers and find myself wanting to jot down a few words to my nearest and dearest (that being you and Andi). I think this is probably a perfectly normal reaction for the new home user such as myself and the hours fly by. In fact, tonight I have done 2 constructive things, and all before Ally starts on the tele. Number 1, I checked out on the internet just exactly what ICQ is and have downloaded info on how to set it up. It sounded far too complicated for me to attempt on my own, it will simply have to wait until I have both you girls here, bottle of wine and loads of fags. Number 2 constructive thing was small amount of work – God, how virtuous do I feel. Very is the answer.

Time for Ally is fast approaching, hope you have good day at work, see you Saturday night, will meet you all there later in the evening.
Love, Nat

Hearty Ministronie
(Ministrony? Minestroney?...)

1 onion, chopped
2 carrots, peeled and chopped
2 celery sticks, chopped
¼ green cabbage, finely shredded
Any green veg lurking in the fridge
400g tin chopped tomatoes
1.2 litres vegetable/chicken stock, from cubes
400g tin cannellini beans, drained and rinsed
100g dried pasta
Salt and freshly ground black pepper

1. Heat a drop of olive oil in a large, lidded saucepan over a medium heat. Add the onion, carrots and celery, season with a little salt and pepper and cook for about 10 minutes, stirring occasionally until the vegetables have softened.

2. Chop any other veg such as broccoli, cauliflower or anything else lurking into small chunks and add to pan. Cook for 10 mins.

3. Tip in the tomatoes and stock. Cover with a lid and bring slowly to the boil. Reduce the heat to a simmer and cook for 15 minutes.

4. Add the beans and pasta and cook for a further 10 minutes, or until the pasta is cooked. Add the cabbage and cook for another 2 minutes. If the soup is too thick, add hot water to reach your preferred consistency.

5. Season to taste with salt and pepper before serving.

For a delicious Bean Soup, make exactly as above but remove cabbage and add tin of kidney beans, chickpeas and tin of green lentils.

November 10, 1999
From Nat:
To: Andi
Subject: Because I wanted to

Dearest Andi,

Had email from someone called 'Matt' – thought I'd found my first Internet stalker, probably someone we picked up the other night in The Brunch Club, but then the old grey matter started to work, and I realized it was your mate Orient Express Matt. I have, of course, emailed him back. It's a fab work avoidance tactic. So nice of you to pass my address on to absolutely everyone you've ever known!

In the end, didn't meet up with Nic tonight, but chatted. I have downloaded load of info on ICQ and how to set it up on my system, but didn't feel brave enough to try without the technical support from my two buds, so it will have to wait until we have a bottle of wine, dinner night.

Sweet dreams, have good day at work.
Love,
Nat

PS Have made contact with big sis in the States and have correct email address, she'd love to hear from you. She says she only gets junk mail and would like some personal correspondence from North London!

November 12, 1999
From: Andi
To: Natalie

You should be so lucky as to pick up some one from the Brunch Club – see, I'm getting into the lingo. Speak to you on Saturday – have a cool evening tonight with the family.

November 17, 1999
From: Natalie
To: Nicole Kissman

Dearest Nic,

We must get our shit together and see and see what is left on the list. I'm in tomorrow night and will try and see if Selfridges have a web site in which I'm sure we could buy direct. The pressie will be from you, me and Johnny, so don't know how much we want to spend. Not a fortune, I hope.

Give me a bell tomorrow. I'm going to be in watching footie – England versus Scotland and then a double bill of Allie. If you wish to drop by, please feel free! Hope you are feeling better, and work is ok. Looking forward to seeing you Friday, no matter what, with bottle of Turkish brandy and sprite.

Will cook something suitable to absorb some of the cheap booze. Not fish risotto for a change.

Loads of love,

Nat

November 18, 1999
From: Nat
To: Nic

How is it that friends always know best? Of course, I got home tonight to lurve messages from Ali. He's not in a good way and leaving for Adrasan tomorrow. I'm so jealous, but want to think of him there with friends rather than miserable in Istanbul.

Unfortunately, Sue won't be in London at all. I really wanted to see her for the same reasons as you. To bring it all to life and to catch up on the gossip. I'm really sad that we won't be there for New Year, but I think that's just selfish.

Let me cook up a storm on Sunday. I'm thinking maybe movie in the afternoon, there are some good ones around. I'm going to Watford on Saturday night to see Steve and Michael and listen to them gloat about their plans in Adrasan. Well, speak to you Sunday.

Love,

Nat

November 18, 1999
From: Natalie
To: Nic

Dearest Nicole,

It's a real shame, but Sue will not be coming to London. Her original plan was to fly out of Gatwick on Tuesday, but she's been ill and had enough. I think she simply wants to get back to her man and to where the sun is still warm and shining. She's flying out of Manchester on Sunday and who can blame her. Given the choice between London and Adrasan right now, I know which one I would choose. Emails from Ali have gone quiet. I spoke to him on Saturday and he was alive, but as he would say 'low in moral' and have not had a message since. That is the problem with receiving wonderful emails every morning and then when you don't you feel a bit … ughh! Think he may have left Istanbul and be in Adrasan.

Well, re Friday, I think as Sue isn't coming, I feel I should go over to Eton Ave and spend the evening with, you know, the long-lost sister. She's going back to the States on Saturday. Re wedding list, should we chat Friday night. I will call or you call at Eton Ave to discuss what's left on the list. Do not know what to wear for wedding, summer wedding stuff is going to be much too cold! Speak to you soon, perhaps Sunday night dinner? Don't feel as though I've seen you in ages and need to catch up with the girls, feeling low and yucky (if you know what I mean?)

Love,
Nat

Risotto

You will need:

1.3l chicken stock
250g pack dessert chestnut mushrooms, sliced
8 rashers smoked streaky bacon, chopped
1 onion, finely chopped
300g arborio rice
1 small glass white wine
50g parmesan, finely grated
Leftover roast chicken, skinned
 and chopped
Handful parsley leaves, chopped

1. Heat a drop of olive oil in a large, lidded saucepan over a medium heat. Start by frying the bacon in half the butter, then add the onion.

2. When they are soft, add the mushrooms and continue to cook for a few mins until soft. Stir through the rice and continue to stir. Add the stock, a ladle full at a time, and keep stirring until the stock has disappeared. (This is where time, care, gentle stoking and attention make all the difference. Hence why the comparison has been made that a man that makes a good risotto, also makes a good lover!)

3. After adding the final ladle of stock, stir through the chicken to reheat.

4. Add the chopped parsley with the Parmesan and remaining butter, leave to rest for a few mins, then stir through and serve.

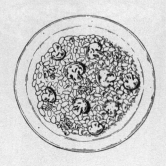

November 22, 1999
From: Nat
To: Andi

Dearest McD,

The bloody novelty tea-pot is disgusting! What can I say, it's horrible and this is what we are meant to give your sister for her wedding present? Oh, what to do?

Actually, had nice evening with Nic. She cooked a fantastic meal, roast chick, pots, parsnips, broccoli, cauliflower … good wine. It was really a day of good food.

Feeling inspired tonight, I have recreated our soup of yesterday, but with different beans. Hope it tastes as good. Penny is out for at least the next 3 days with really bad throat and other members of staff also ill, so loads of cover to sort out. Nightmare, but also busy and stimulating. I hope your course was good, or rather the first day!

Had news from Adrasan, Ali is climbing mountains and riding bikes, sounds pretty good to me. Sister obviously rang Myrtle to say Nat is buggering off to Turkey, and so Myrt, the true romantic, rang me to say can I buy your flight. I am going to look into it tomorrow, will definitely be back for New Years. I'm really looking forward to the prospect of Cardiff.

For now, soup beckoning.
Love,
Nat

December 1999

December 9, 1999
From: Nic
To: Natalie
Re: How are you friend?

I know, I feel like I haven't spoken to you in months, it was only the weekend. I know you're seeing Andi tonight, I caught up with her last night. What are you doing tomorrow night, if I promise not to go to sleep? Also, what are you doing on Sunday night? It's Xmas time at mine, putting up my tree. I need yours and Andi's artistic flair. What did we ever do without email, we would be lost! Love you lots, let me know and have fun with Andi tonight - I have my Xmas party. Speak to you later.
Nic

December 9, 1999
From : Natalie
To: Nic

Days flying by and don't seem to have time to stop and think. I hope you are around tonight/tomorrow. I know you are away Saturday, but feel the need to touch base with girls.

December 9, 1999
From: Natalie
To: Nic
Re: Friend, I'm fine!

Dearest Nic,

It seems like a lifetime. Andi told me you have do tonight. Have fab time and pace yourself. What about a lazy Friday night, I could cook, or I think perhaps it's Andi's turn! We will chat tonight! Yes, yes, yes to Sunday night. Have you got Xmas carols so we can really get in the mood? Love you loads. Only 1 more day to go. Ring me tomorrow when you get home and make sure you leave at a reasonable time.

Natalie

December 9, 1999
From: Andi
To: Natalie
Re: Ce soir

I can't work out the time that this was written – you are either up bloody late on Wednesday night or up far far too early on Thursday morning. You're not getting addicted, are you ??? Howz about going out for risotto? We could pop along to Criteria near Cannonbury for a good risotto and bottle of wine – no washing up, either which has to be a bonus. Call me when you get in. Good luck with the report writing. Tell 'em they only get a red star … gold stars are only for people that don't say the 'C' word.

Lorra love,

Andi

December 9, 1999
From: Natalie
To: Andi
Re: Ce soir

Dearest,

What is this about ELFbowl virus, anyway couldn't figure out how to open attachment, so deleted the whole thing. I can just imagine getting home on Jan 1, 2000 to find computer small pile of ash on table. Week fluctuating between fab and crap, but it's Thursday and feeling pretty good. Are we on for risotto chez toi? I will bring over your wine from Tom, okay? I will probably be home at about 4 ish as have loads of reports to do.

December 12, 1999
From: Natalie
To: Andi
Subject: A cup of courage - Heartstrings

You have just received an animated greeting card from Nat @ Blue Mountain Cards…

December 13, 1999
From: Andi
To: Natalie
Re: A cup of courage – Heartstrings

I LOVE IT! I'm going to bring my laptop home, so that I can mess around too. See you later this week, are you free any night?

December 13, 1999
From: Natalie
To: Andi
Re: Bowl of soup?

Dearest McD,
If you fancy coming over and playing on mine, do. I was just sent a bunch of virtual roses from Jac and Simon today. Will send Ali a bunch for his birthday tomorrow, don't forget. What is closer, will call you once I'm off email.
Love,
Nat

December 14, 1999
From: Natalie
To: Andi
Re: theatre

We are just such cultural buffs, theatre sounds fab. I hope I haven't seen it, it's not about petty criminals in the East End, is it? See you at weekend, want update re Big. When are you meeting, how are you feeling etc. Let me know all – have just spoke to Nic about trying to get her one night next week for our Christmas do together – Wednesday or Thursday?
For now,
Love Nat

Smoked Fish Risotto

You will need:

60g butter
400g skinless smoked fish fillets
   (eg. coley, cod, blue-eye, ling),
   cut into 3 cm cubes
40g frozen peas
1.25 litres fish stock
1 onion, finely chopped
1 clove garlic, crushed
330g arborio rice
2 tablespoons lemon juice
1 tablespoon chopped fresh parsley
1 tablespoon chopped fresh chives
1 tablespoon chopped fresh dill

1. Melt half the butter in a pan. Add the fish in batches and fry over medium-high heat for 3 minutes, or until the fish is just cooked through. Remove from the pan and set aside.

2. Pour the fish stock into another pan, bring to the boil, cover and keep at simmering point.

3. To the first pan, add the remaining butter, onion and garlic and cook over medium heat for 3 minutes, or until the onion is tender. Add the rice and stir to coat, then add a ladle of the fish stock and cook, stirring constantly, over low heat until all the stock has been absorbed. Continue adding a ladle of stock at a time until all the stock has been added and the rice is translucent, tender and creamy. Throw in the frozen peas and cook for 3 mins until cooked through.

4. Stir in the lemon juice and herbs. Add the fish and stir gently.

December 15, 1999
From: Andi
To: Natalie
Subj: How exciting!

Mum's just called and mentioned that she spoke to you about my Xmas pressie – a new computer! Does this mean that we never have to speak again, and we can have virtual bowls of soup each night, from the comfort of our own flats? Cool beans, Nat. Thanks for all the positive things you said to Ma – it obviously worked. Ciao,
Andi

December 15, 1999
From: Natalie
To: Nic
RE: Work

Dearest Nic,
Must be like a kick in the teeth after so many days out. You will cope and just think only about a week to go til your hols kick in. Mailed Andi re night to meet up next week, you guys chat and let me know, Wednesday or Thursday.
Love Nat
See you on Sunday for fab lunch

December 16, 1999
From: Natalie
To: Nic
Re: Yes to Thursday!

Thursday sounds fab! At yours is a good idea, mine is about as Christmassy as something not at all!
Love Nat

December 16, 1999
From: Nic
To: Natalie

Excellent, mine is far too Christmassy for one, hence the need to share, looking forward to it! What day are you in town next week, can't remember? I'm going to go home via Oxford Street and Xmas shopping, so I'll check out what's on offer as well.
Speak to you later,
Nic

December 16, 1999
From: Andi
To: Natalie
Subj: Butterfly City

Nat, I'm out both tonight and tomorrow – staff do each night. Tomorrow night, I'm also meeting up with Big!!!!! Can't wait and will tell you all when I see you. Can you find out what Penny's mobile number is, so that I can call when we're out. Maybe we could meet up, but we'll have to see how it goes. Can't wait to tell you all about my computer delivery.
TTFN
Andi xxx

December 16, 1999
From: Natalie
To: Andi
Re: Ce soir

Dearest McD,

I'm so pleased you think PC is a good pressie. I thought it was a brill idea and was struggling trying not to tell you the other night. I am dead with exhaustion, only stayed for a few drinks last night and in fact left with another teacher, so not exactly the first to go. Will be free of kids by 2pm today – what a good feeling that will be! Will be home early and making cards, if you fancy dins. You may be busy entertaining, so mail and let me know.

Lentil Soup

You will need:

3 Tbsp olive oil
1 medium onion, chopped
1 medium carrot, grated
3 cloves garlic, finely chopped
3 Tbsp tomato paste
1 red pepper
1 tsp sugar
180 g red lentils
1 ltrs veg stock
salt and pepper
1 lemon
small handful freshly chopped flat leaf parsley

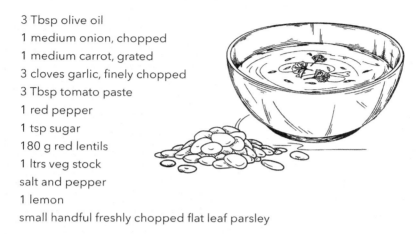

1. Heat a large heavy bottomed pot over medium heat. Add the oil, onion and carrot. Sauté, stirring regularly, until softened but not coloured, 8-10 minutes.

2. Add the garlic, tomato paste, chopped red pepper and sugar. Cook until the tomato and pepper have been cooked through and mixed well with the other ingredients, 1-2 minutes. Add the lentils and give it all a good stir.

3. Add the stock and season to taste with salt and pepper. Bring to a boil, stir to stop it sticking and pop on a lid and turn the heat down to low. Leave to simmer until the lentils are cooked through and starting to fall apart, around 15 minutes.

4. Whizz with a stick blender. Add lemon juice and chopped parsely.

December 16, 1999
From: Nic
To: Andi, Natalie

Girls,
Thursday is best for me. I would love to have you over to mine. Let me know,
hope the week is going well.

December 17, 1999
From: Natalie
To: Andi
Re: Catching up

Dearest McD,
You may well have a late night on Friday, so shan't call you early. Am off to
Dalston to get ticket, hair done, market, so will probably be back 11-12 ish. If
you don't have plans and that suits, then let me know.
Love,
Nat

December 20, 1999
From: Natalie
To: Nic
Re: Shopping

Dearest Nic,
Got home and don't quite know what to make of that play! See you tomorrow
at 11.30 by the gloves in good ol' John Lewis. Have a good meeting.
Love,
Nat

December 21, 1999
From: Natalie
To: Andi
Subject: About last night ...

Dearest Andi,
Hope you had a wonderful night. I have been conducting my cyber relationship
for the last few hours. I hope we get on as well when we see each other as we
do on the net.
Love, Nat

December 22, 1999
From: Andi
To: Natalie
Re: About last night ...

Last night was great ... lots of kissing, a great meal and exchange of Christmas pressies – what more would a girl want (other than a great s**g!) I was cool ... no mention of when are we going to meet, what are we doing etc. but lots of great chat and meandering down memory lane. Strange though it may be, I actually feel on top of this and almost know that not only will we never be together 100%, but that I almost don't want that. I feel weird putting this in writing, as once said, you have to admit your feelings, but perhaps Big has been wise in holding back. There is no denying the strength of feeling – I truly love the man and I know the feeling is mutual – but whether we could ever make our two lives really come together is another question. A little something to mull over.

I'm out tonight at a trendy restaurant – Pharmacy – with all the Directors of Sales from our UK hotels. It should be quite a laugh, but I'd far rather be with the Portman clan. Have a wonderful time tonight and give Lucia a big kiss from me. What are you up to on Thursday evening? Not sure whether I'm seeing the ol' Pops, but would love to catch up.

December 24, 1999
From: Natalie
To: Andi, Nic
Re: Thanks girls!

What a great night, I got home and enjoyed listening to my CD and looking at my pressies before finally passing out feeling a bit woozy and dehydrated (could it be too much and too many drinks consumed?)
Thinking of you both today at work. I'm sure I don't need to tell you both to take it easy and leave early, and as for McD, just have a great lunch with Big. Hmmm, gossip to be had in the new year.
Lots of love,
Nat

January 2000

January 4, 2000
From: Andi
To: Natalie
Subject : Welcome home

So, this is it – I'm online and we never need to see each other again! Here's to many virtual bowls of soups … delighted you had a good time in Adrasan with Ali baby. Don't get too stressed about not 'opening up' – he knows you well and will understand why you were not full of the usual Nat-joys of spring. See you tomorrow night for a steaming bowl of soup.
Sleep tight to you and Lucia.
Big snog.
Andi

From: Andi
To: Natalie
Subj: Luscious soup

Thanks, Nat, for a great evening – just what every girl would want, even if we did just talk about sex rather than find the men to act out the nipple test with. Hope the chat with the tutor tomorrow goes well – don't expect all your questions to be answered. Big kiss,
Andi

January 5, 2000
From: Natalie
To: Andi
Re: Fab sofa session

Dearest McD,

Good to have a bit of quality down time with you on the sofa tonight (it sounds positively smutty) Oh the joys of sharing, I am hanging out Lucy's washing, what bliss! We will be wearing each others knickers next, not!

January 6, 2000
From: Andi
To: Natalie

Before your dad runs out and get you a new printer, Dad is offering his old one for free - check it out this weekend as he is also giving away his old photocopier. It just needs a new ribbon. Sale of the century!

January 6, 2000
From: Natalie
To: Andi

Bargains to be had for all at Willes Road. Sounds pretty damned good to me. The McD crowd are a fab bunch to know!

January 7, 2000
From: Nic
To: Natalie
Subject: Removals

How's it being back, urghhhhh! I'm sure. Lovely to have you back though! I'm out tonight, lovely meal somewhere nice, not been told where and no, not with the man whose name I won't mention but with Nigel and Wayne from work. If you need help in the morning though, give me a shout. Love you lots,
Nic

January 9, 2000
From: Natalie
To: Andi
Re: I rang!

Dearest McD,

After all your prompting, I finally picked up the phone and rang. Ali sounded surprised to hear from me. It seems that he is living in the new factory and, at the moment, there's no phone line, he has not received my mail, as he can't access his internet or use ICQ. I told him part of my plan, the leaving the job. He said that he is now looking at a solid period of work to complete and is waiting for his studio flat to be built above the new workshop. So, he mentioned, unprompted, coming over to London when I finish work, that would be wonderful. He sounds envious of the life we have here, the bowls of soup and chat each night, that is the price he is paying. We finished the conversation with him saying "love me" and I replied, "I do."

Do you think that is an improvement for me? A bit more open and all that, I was shaking like a leaf just picking up the phone and calling. Isn't it crap that someone can make me, you, all of us, behave in such a fashion?

Well, I feel a bit better now, still a bit sick in the stomach, but better. I hope I will have sweet dreams tonight and wake up feeling ready to tackle the horrors of money at the unit.

For now, sweets, thanks for being such a fab mate and putting up with all the wittering.
Love,
Nat

Roast chicken
with all the trims

You will need:

freshly ground black pepper
1 large free range chicken
olive oil
1 bulb garlic , cut in half horizontally
1 lemon
1 small bunch fresh thyme
sea salt

1. Preheat the oven to 200°C/400°F/gas 6.

2. Place the chicken in a roasting tray and drizzle with a good lug of olive oil. Slice the lemon in half and, with the thyme sprigs, stuff into the cavity of the chicken. Add the garlic to the tray and roast in the oven for 1 hour and 30 minutes or until the chicken is cooked and golden brown (when pierced with a knife, the juices should run clear).

3. Leave the chicken to rest for 10 minutes

4. To make the gravy - Stir in a couple of tablespoons of flour and some stock with a glug of white wine until thickened, and strain through a sieve.

5. Serve with roast potatoes, cauliflower cheese, carrot and swede mush and peas.

January 9, 2000
From: Andi
To: Natalie
Subj: Well done!

I'm proud of you! Don't you feel better for it?? If you'd just have picked up the phone earlier this week, you would have realized that he doesn't have access to email. You tonker! I'm delighted that he is talking about coming over. Does the solid period of work mean that he is burying his head over the next month or so? He should be envious of the life we have here – it's very special and I treasure it. Neither of us should take for granted how lucky we are to have someone that we can witter on to, to such a huge extent. The number of times over the last 2 years I must have bored you to tears with complicated tales of Big, but still you listen and give me the encouragement I yearn for. Thanks. Nat. Ok, enough mooch from McD and time for bed. Sleep with a smile on your face and in your heart (OK a tiny mooch to close off with!!!)
Love,
Andi

January 10, 2000
From: Andi
To: Natalie
Re: I feel poorly

Nat - I've taken the day off work and am still in bed. I feel really nauseous, had funny tummy and feel faint. All in all, not so hot. Doubt it was the lentil soup though! Call me later,
Andi

From: Natalie
To: Andi
Re: Thanks for cheesy mail!

You are such an emotional chick, but it's true – we'd have gone quite mad by now, if it weren't for having each other around the last few years. But you know, I will not be away for long and then some of the chats will simply take place in a different location. Anyway, wherever I end up, you may fancy a holiday there, and of course I will be home for the big 30, really wouldn't miss it for the world.
Love,
Nat – will let you know how all the agents go and if we are talking ridiculously big wanga!

January 11, 2000
From: Natalie
To: Nic

Dearest Kissman,
Don't know if you are back there today. If you are, I'm thinking of you and just want to drop you a cheesy line to let you know you don't have to go through all of this alone if you don't want to. If, on the other hand, you are still at home, ignore this mail. I will tell you later.
Lots of love,
Nat

January 11, 2000
From: Nic
To: Natalie
Re: Friends

Back at work in body if not mind. Thanks for being there. If I didn't think you were, it would be even worse, if possible. Gotta sort myself out. Speak to you later.

January 12, 2000
From: Natalie
To: Nic, Andi
Re: Friends!

Just a little bit merry but just a "Cheesy" word to say "aren't friends fab!"
You two are certainly friends in a million, even when we aren't on the best form, we manage to entertain, listen to, commiserate … with each other. That is the most important thing in life. Where would I be without your patience, and all the rest (have big black fly on the screen, it has just fallen off)
So love being able to catch up with you at moment's notice mid-week.
Whatever else, I will only be gone for short time, couldn't survive long without you both.
Enough cheesing, save it for another day and more booze.
Love you both,
Nat

January 14, 2000
From: Natalie
To: Andi

Thanks for cheesy message yesterday, what is this, are we trying to outdo each other? Just quick question, do Scott and Al know about tomorrow night, as I have not called them and do not have Johnny's number. I will be at Eton Ave around 6ish, if you have the chance, call them if they do not know, as it would be a shame if they can't make it.

Sent Flo soppy card, we can call her tonight from Eton Ave.

See you tonight.

Love,

Nat

January 16, 2000
From: Natalie
To: Andi
Re: It's my birthday and I'll cry if I want to

Dearest McD,

Am currently emailing your dad on ICQ. He is off to bed now, but tells me there are lots of orphanages in Bulgaria. I would like to pick his brains one night online and get some ideas about whether it may be interesting for a couple of months. The rose is absolutely wonderful, you have really made this a fantastic weekend for me and are the best friend anyone could ever hope for. Enough of the cheese, please.

I have tidied the flat, checked messages and opened email. Not a word from Ali. I feel hurt and confused, how can he tell me he loves me and then forget so easily. Are people really so fickle, is it simply that he is so busy he hasn't time to think of me ever and doesn't know what day it is or time? That is what I would like to think, but I am really doubting him, he of all people. I would be so disappointed if he turns out not to be the man I thought he was, perhaps I turned out not be the woman he thought I was. Enough soul searching for tonight, it's not the day for it.

Thanks again for everything, did you get the cabinet sorted?

Love,

Nat

January 17, 2000
From: Natalie
To: Andi, Nic

Dearest All,

Thanks for being the "usual suspects" and helping me to celebrate my birthday. I really had a wonderful time and hope you all enjoyed yourselves too. I know I did and have got the bags to prove it and the dodgy stomach, icky feeling and all the other symptoms of not enough sleep and too much of the lovely liquid stuff along with all those fags. All I can say now is sleep well to the dilly ha has and the same to the cha cha's. (Tom, I will have to explain this one to you another time) and hope the lumps are all ok.

Love from very mature 30 year old – Natalie Portman

January 17, 2000
From: Andi
To: Natalie Portman
Re: Thanks!

So beautifully put! I think that the binkle has now been superseded by the cha cha! Have a cool week. Looking at my diary, I'm out most nights, so I'll mail the CV to you, so you get the hard copy quickly. I'll speak to you by email.
Love,
Andi

January 21, 2000
From: Nat
To: Nic

If all goes well, I should be flitting off to Aldeburgh with the Blanchett Chickster tonight in her not so sprightly car, should be interesting. If you are not busy, what about spot of dins chez moi Sunday night, I have asked Andi over to go through my CV and I would appreciate any advice from the Kissman Business Woman of the Year! If you get a call from me tomorrow, then you know weekend plans have ended in disaster around my ankles.

Love,

Nat

January 26, 2000
From: Natalie
To: Nic, Andi
Re: Brie (very good squishy one)

How are you both, I really should tone down my cheerful, happy thoughts.
I do apologise, I just can't help the welling up happy feelings each day. Off
to supermarket to buy choice of sanitary wear for today's PSHE lesson – just
imagine the chaos! Tonight, dinner at Eton Ave, presents have finally arrived
for Christmas and Birthday from the States, so also stuff to open. I will be in
tomorrow if anyone needs/wants to talk/see me.
Have fabby dooby day, Nat.

January 26, 2000
From: Nic
To: Natalie
Re: Weekend

I want to finish at your time of day!!! Please!!! Have a good one. Lol.
Nic

January 27, 2000
From: Natalie
To: Nic, Andi
Re: Chevre (tangy not too goaty)

It's already Thursday and week is flying by. Told staff I was going, they took
it all in their stride to shouts of 'you bitch' … I think lots of jealous people. In
fact, yesterday was one of the best days so far there, isn't it odd that once you
are leaving, you can actually start to enjoy it all. Will be in tonight, doing CV
before deadline. Have found good contact in Romania with very small home
for handicapped children. I am absolutely gutted about my watch. I think there
must have been some kind of chip in the glass for that to happen. Can't believe
it after all the trouble everyone went to. Any top suggestions of what to do?
Looking forward to Saturday night, girls night out and all that – chat later.
Love,
Nat

Parsnip soup

You will need:

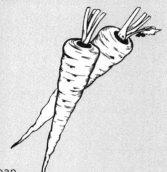

1 tbsp olive oil
2 garlic cloves, finely chopped
600g parsnips – medium cubes
½ tsp cumin
1 litre vegetable stock
200ml double cream
salt and freshly ground black pepper

1. Heat the oil in a heavy-based saucepan over a medium heat. Add the garlic and parsnips and fry for 4–5 minutes, stirring occasionally, until coloured. Add the cumin powder and fry for 1 minute.

2. Pour in the stock, stir and bring to a simmer. Cook with the lid on for 12–15 minutes, or until the parsnips are tender.

3. Remove the soup from the heat and blitz with a stick blender until smooth. Return to the heat, stir in the cream and heat through. Season to taste with salt and pepper.

February 2000

February 1, 2000
From: Natalie
To: Andi, Nic
Subj: Edam

Dearest both,
Edam just about sums up how I feel this morning, red on the outside and hard and waxy inside. Looking forward to leaving school for home visits at 12.30 and then not having to return. Very lazy person that I am. Have a simply splendiferous Tuesday, enjoy all that it has to offer!
Love,
Nat

February 1, 2000
From: Andi
To: Natalie
Re: Edam

A little waxy on the inside… Hmmm… sounds a little dodgy… have you thought about seeing a doctor????
Enjoy your lazy afternoon at home. By the way, the fax went off successfully this morning.
Love,
Andi

February 2, 2000
From: Natalie
To: Nic, Andi
Re: Halloumi

Dearest both,
Hard and squeaky as opposed to waxy, but thought it was appropriate in the light of pending interview for a job in Istanbul. Yesterday also brought another wonderful contact on the Romania front, the Met Police. They are running an aid convoy out there, leaving London May 15 and I am hoping to tag along. Getting to know all the people involved in aid agencies there and developing useful contacts. All bloody exciting!
The really important thing is that ER starts tonight, and I am wondering whether Kissman would like to feed me a little light dinner and let me drool over new gorgeous doctor? Andi, will you be busy? So, mail me girls and let me know, who, what is around tonight.
Love,
Nat

February 2, 2000
From: Nic
To: Andi, Natalie
Re: Halloumi

Progress on the Romania front sounds very exciting, so many options. Can I meet all those lovely policemen!!! Would love to catch with you both tonight, I can hit M&S on the way home and do a big salad, let me know. Also seeing Cate B for coffee this afternoon to look at finances, hopefully take watch back as well. Speak to you both later.
Nic

February 3, 2000
From: Natalie
To: Nic, Andi
Re: The cheesiest of the lot "Philadelphia"

I feel a huge emotional gush this morning. I apologise in advance, but you will soon get the gist of why. Yes, he is coming! Off to get visa at weekend and is going to try to get flight on Friday and stay til following Sunday. He is obviously unaware that only talking very infrequently is a bit difficult for me and that will be a conversation to be had when we are together. He really seems to think that the thought of me is what is keeping him going and that since we last spoke, he has finished jobs, done loads because he has been motivated by the thought of coming over here. I wish I could have felt or telepathically known this, I think it's the nature of insecure women to demand constant attention, not short sharp bursts of quality.

Hmm, told him I have an interview on the Saturday, but am not planning to tell him it's for a job in Istanbul, perhaps after the fact I may but ... you know me, always like to keep some things hidden.

I am in tonight cooking for Penny and Terrence and no doubt drinking too much, smoking too much, and staying up too late. Friday is always a breeze to get through.

For now, sorry I am cheesingly, disgustingly happy – tiptoe through the tulips ... la-di-da ... doe a deer a female ... and all of that cheesy musical stuff.

Love you both (true cheese) – yuck, will make myself sick soon!

Nat

XX

February 3, 2000
From: Nic
To: Natalie
CC: Andi

Bloody hell! And hallelujah all in the same breath.
Yippeeee! Very pleased for you. LOL
Nic

February 4, 2000
From: Natalie
To: Nic, Andi
Re: Dairy Lee

Dearest both,

As you can see, I have now hit the low point in terms of cheese, delicious processed, am rather partial. Feeling a little, hmm, delicate this morning. Penny is just beginning to surface and although Terrance did go home, he crashed here first. Sofa session for me.

Looking forward to early dinner with parents at Stokie's finest, yum yum, and then early to bed. Anyone up to little local scene tomorrow – Boots, market, Mark 1, coffee in … get the picture? Too tired to gush, but very quiet and smiley this morning, even tho ugh bloody knackered.

Love, Nat

February 4, 2000
From: Andi
To: Nic, Natalie
Re: Dairy Lee

I don't know where you find the energy or brain power to write these messages in the morning – I love it, so please don't stop. Let's meet up in the morning and I'll hit the West End in the afternoon or even on Sunday. I have a whole weekend of nothing – yippee! Catch you both tomorrow – I will no doubt need lots of toast and coffee after tonight's extravaganza, so beware!

February 5, 2000
To: Andi
From: Natalie
Re: Saturday morning catch up

Dearest McD,

I have a few chores to do this morning – you know tidy the flat, go to Boots and then back here for 12. I have two lots of people coming round to the view the flat for the 2nd time and Brooks seems to think one/two offers may come in. So, I will be done in Dalston about 10.30 and if it's okay with you, I will pop round, ring first or you come round here when you are up. Looks like it's going to be a bloody gorgeous day, perhaps we could venture out and about.

OK, sweet stuff, catch up with you later.

Nat

February 7, 2000
From: Nic
To: Natalie, Andi
Re: Camembert

Definitely on for the soup, moaning to Andi this morning that the clothes are far too tight, trying not to sink into depression over it, keep thinking PMA, trouble is think I have PMT as well.
Catch you later.

February 7, 2000
From: Natalie
To: Andi, Nic
Re: Camembert

Dearest both,
Monday is never the best day for cheese, I always wake up thinking how will I get through the week, but here I am, faithfully mailing you with today's missive. Already looking forward to getting home tonight, putting on the pot of soup and I think opening a bottle of wine and relaxing into the week. Looking forward to any soup takers tonight (know you are busy, Andi!) It will be a variation on the roast parsnip theme! Don't worry, Nic, it will be healthy filling, nutritious and … I will be home disgustingly early!
Love,
Nat

February 7, 2000
From: Andi
To: Nic, Natalie
Subj: I've screwed up

Guys, I've just checked out my diary and have completely screwed up. I thought I was away the weekend of 18/19 Feb, but in fact I'm around and am 25/26 Feb in Berlin. Two choices – I either miss out on Aldeburgh altogether (boo hoo) or maybe take Monday 21 off and join you – just don't want to crowd you, Nat. Sorry about this. Let me know whether you are taking the cottage on Crag Path or by the town steps and what dates you are working around. I'm out with Jules tonight but will call you both from the mobile.
Catch you later!
Love,
Andi

February 8, 2000
From: Andi
To: Natalie
Re: Primula spread

If, indeed, you open up this message and it's not even 5pm, I will hate you! Soooo wish that I was currently at home, with the heating on, still in my PJ's, mug of coffee in hand and watching crap TV. But alas, I'm about to go into our weekly meeting to hear more corporate BS. Catch you later – I may pop in for coffee if I finish dinner with George at a reasonable time.
Lots of love from a happy McD, who knows that in 8 days, she will have a naked man in her bed!!

February 8, 2000
From: Andi
To: Natalie, Nic
Subject: I'm free tonight!

My dinner with George has cancelled tonight, so do you fancy sharing a bowl of soup or salad at a freshly cleaned Bethune Road?

February 8, 2000
From: Nic
To: Andi, Natalie
Re: I'm free tonight

Sounds like an excellent idea to me, being cheeky, what are the chances of a lift home as well! I'll call you when I get out of my next meeting, appx 3.30.
Lol.
Nic

Moules in cream sauce

You will need:

1.75kg mussels
1 garlic clove, finely chopped
2 shallots, finely chopped
15g butter
Bay leaf
100ml dry white wine
120ml double cream
handful of parsley leaves,
  coarsely chopped
crusty bread or chips, to serve

1. Wash the mussels under plenty of cold, running water. Discard any open ones that won't close when lightly squeezed.

2. Pull out the beards from between the tightly closed shells and knock off any barnacles with a large knife. Give the mussels another quick rinse to remove any little pieces of shell.

3. Soften the garlic and shallots in the butter with the bay leaf in a large pan big enough to take all the mussels - it should only be half full.

4. Add the mussels and wine, turn up the heat, then cover and steam them open in their own juices for 3-4 minutes. Give the pan a good shake every now and then.

5. Remove the bay leaf, add the cream and chopped parsley and remove from the heat.

6. Spoon into four large warmed bowls and serve with lots of crusty bread and thin chips.

February 8, 2000
From: Natalie
To: Nic, Andi
Re: Primula spread

Dearest girls,
Andi, you are so right, how could we have forgotten the soufle? We are so sorry, grovel, grovel, kiss your feet .. think soufle starter, followed by crab/lobster niçoise, is top idea and then totally indulge with something unbearably gooey, chocolaty, sticky stuff a la Nic. Getting very excited by the prospect, will no doubt have further discussions with you over the week re the best ingredients … well, hard to be cheesy on bloody wet Tuesday, but do you know what, girls, I can be home by about 3 ish, you know these home visit days! Bloody doss. Still can manage a little of the cheese stuff, love you both loads, have a gorgeous Tuesday and I need some cheese suggestions, am really scraping the barrel.

February 9, 2000
From: Natalie
To: Nic, Andi
Re: Cheese of the day – cottage cheese

To the Stamford wives,
Low fat cheese is the way forward after seeing some of those shots last night. I think all fat ugly shots of should be burnt in a ritual bonfire with us dancing naked around it. A most amusing Tuesday night, top soup, cheese, the usual … Beautiful morning and amazingly enough, the rain has stopped pouring in through the roof at last. Have session with Rosa tonight and curry tomorrow – hmm, fab sounding social. Enjoy today, mail later.

··

February 9, 2000
From: Andi
To: Natalie
Subj: What, no cheese!

··

What is this … no cheese this morning? And after lengthy discussions about cheese counters etc??? Just kidding – I only just realized that there was no message from you this morning. I've checked out dates and would love to go over and visit Cath with you. Ideally, I only want to spend max 3 nights. Thanks for acting as travel agent on this one.
Speak to you later.
Love, Andi

··

February 10, 2000
From: Nic
To: Natalie
Re: Primula spread... dairy lee slice, Sarah Lee gateaux

··

Sorry, love. Very poor of me, but very busy day yesterday. My turn to be in a surprisingly good mood this morning, bearing in mind how foul it is outside, must be the prospect of a long weekend ahead. Looking forward to an evening in tonight, clear up the place. Good night out last night, drinks with Nig!

··

February 10, 2000
From: Natalie
To: Nic, Andi
Re: Primula spread

··

Dearest grills,
Is that bacon or sausage? What do you mean no cheesy mail, Ms McD? I consider primula spread to be pretty bloody cheesy. Oh why, oh why, do I have to go to work today. It's bloody foul, wind, rain, not a day for doing learning, or even trying to do it. Tired and just want to go back to bed, not helped by prospect of pub ce soir in East London, but I will have to be sober judge as will have car. Looking forward to big time pamper tomorrow.
Look forward to loving mail from you both (Kissman!)
Nat

February 10, 2000
From: Andi
To: Natalie

Really weird, but yesterday's cheesy mail popped up at about 4pm. I just missed you in the morning, dearest. That's all! Tis a pissy, yucky day, but life feels quite peachy regardless. Had a scrummy dinner at China House last night (smaller, nicer version of Wagamama plus a bar where you can smoke!) with the team and had a real giggle. Just about to go into a meeting, out for lunch and dinner. I'm getting fat! And flying tomorrow morning to Scotland. Will call you from the bonnie land over the weekend.
Looking forward to our Valentine dinner, a session of last week's ER and a good girlie evening.
Love ya,
Andi

February 11, 2000
From: Nic
To: Natalie, Andi
Re: Classic lemon cheesecake

My cheerful phase lasted as long as I expected, seconds! Was the lull before the depressive storm, sorry Nat, will try and sort myself out before tonight. Major period onslaught is to blame! Andi, hope you found the wrap ok, you're gonna look gorgeous as ever, have fun! Nat, clever move with the cheesecake, provides the perfect association for a move towards alternative cake morning mails, more choices, very subtle, impressed! If you pick up mail before you phone, moules sound fantastic, need to get some cream for the sauce, double for the amaretto, suddenly cheering up, wonder why! Love the sound of indulgence. Longest mail ever written – obviously feeling the need to communicate with loved ones and ease away the depressive mood. That or I've taken too many Solpadeine as usual – floaty, floaty, appears to be helping though, so will throw myself into work now in case the moment passes too quickly.
Speak to you later,
Nic

February 11, 2000
From: Natalie
To: Andi, Nic
Subject: Classic lemon cheesecake

Girls, do you think cheesecake counts or not, just felt like it this morning.
I am nothing if not a risk taker as demonstrated with new strand veering
dangerously close to the puds department.
Well, you two sound cheerful, why? I too am looking forward to romantic
night with you both, but before then looking forward to a weekend of utter
indulgence, starting tonight with the Kissman. I am suggesting moules, will go
shopping after work, but ring you beforehand to consult on tonight's luxury
ingredients.
Must dash, 7 mails to respond to this morning, it's too many! Running late,
need to clean bits of flat as showing today and tired after night with McD. Have
a wonderful time, call – luv ya both loads.
Nat

February 13, 2000
From: Natalie
To: Nic
Subject: Love potion – from Monsieur Gorgonzola

You have just received an animated greeting card from Monsieur Gorgonzola.
You will see the personal greeting at bluemountain.com!

February 14, 2000
From: Natalie
To: Nic, Andi
Re: Tiramisu (ricotta cheese)

Dearest Valentine girlies, Hope you get loads of cards today. Wonder who you
will both be having dinner with tonight.
Love, Nat

February 15, 2000
From: Nic
To: Andi, Natalie
Re: Chocolate, white chocolate and cream!

Ditto, ditto, ditto, fab evening. Just had a fantastic thought for Andi to use up the mousse cake gateaux.
Recipe as follows :- Allow cake to warm to room temperature. Cut into slices (the whole 7 inches). Put on furry hand cuffs. Strip your loved one naked. I leave the rest to your imagination, much richer than honey!!! And much more exciting. Dirty suggestions for the day over, best get back to work. I will leave you both to dreams of your respective men,LOL to you both,
Nic

February 15, 2000
From: Andi
To: Nic, Natalie
Re: Choc, white choc and cream!

It really was a fab night, and yep, felt like a great big chocolate blob today. Starvation diet today so that the tummy doesn't hang over the edge of the bed tomorrow! Love you both tonnes, as you know, and long for our next binge together. If I could hug you both now I would ... virtual kisses and all that ...
Andi

February 15, 2000
From: Natalie
To: Andi, Nic

Sorry, can't even think cheese this morning after my chocolate overdose last night. It was an absolutely fab dinner of the very best variety. Too much of everything and presents to go home with. Slept like a huge slab of Nic's ultra-rich chocolate cake, struggling with idea of living and functioning today, will have to get on, face the day and eat some fruit to offset excess of last night. Thanks a million for wonderful night – the best.
Nat XX

February 15, 2000
From: Natalie
To: Andi
Re: Chocolate and serving suggestions

Dearest McD,

Well, the handcuffs and slices of chocolate goo may well do the trick. What more could the man want, the perfect combo, sex and chocolate all rolled into one! Yum, have told all how wonderful last night's dinner was with you guys even down to the heart shaped biscuits. No one else even with loved ones seemed to have half the fun we had.

Hope your line at home is up and running, so you can collect mail and then, of course, send mail with all juicy sordid parts of the whole day. No doubt Nic will be ringing you with serving suggestions for chocolate, cake and cuffs throughout the day! I will be in for ER tonight and being at one with the sofa. If you can ring and tell all. Again – fab night –

Love, Nat

PS S&M can't make it on Sunday, a real shame but they are away for the weekend, so it will be the usual suspects and Tom Cruise, help … suddenly makes me nervous without the boys to be giggling and providing suitable innuendo at all occasions.

February 16, 2000
From: Natalie
To: Nic, Andi
Re: Bread and butter pudding with cream cheese

Dearest both,

I hope you like the cunning way in which I am still manoeuvring into the pudding area, while keeping the savory cheese theme riding on the wave. God, how the brain functions first thing in the morning.

Quickie simply to say I am in tonight, making soup. Assume Andi will be busy or unable to walk, or doing John Wayne impressions. So, Kissman, it's over to you. Bowl of soup on offer if you wish.

Love,

Nat

February 16, 2000
From: Nic
To: Natalie
Re: Bread and butter pud

*You're on. As I am at Liverpool Street today, I am going to make a big effort to
go to the gym, fingers crossed!*
Will ring you when I get in.
Nic

February 17, 2000
From: Natalie
To: Andi
Re: Tonight

I will be in Bierodrome from about 5 on. I will no doubt have dumped the
car somewhere and, by the stage you arrive, be pacing myself. So, come and
save me from myself and everyone else there as early as you like. I am looking
forward to tonight, it's always good to meet new people and it will be another
person on the IOM who we can hang out with and drink with. Also wanted to
say if you are around on Saturday night, I would love you to be around. I feel as
though I would like you and Ali to get to know each other better. So, simply if
you are around, it would be fab.
See you tonight – so what did you decide to wear?

February 17, 2000
From: Natalie
To: Nic, Andi
Re: Morning chocolate bomb with mascarpone

Dearest girls,
Thanks for listening to my gripes last night, unusual for chirpy Nat to be feeling
so blue. Spoke to Ali last night, he has booked his ticket and is collecting it today,
he is definitely coming on Saturday afternoon and staying until the following
Sunday afternoon. What am I complaining about? Spoilt brat that I am.
Thanks for chocolate, bit too early even for me at 7.30 – will no doubt tuck in
tonight in a drunken stupor.
For now, must dash.
Love,
Nat

**February 17, 2000
From: Andi
To: Nic, Natalie
RE: Morning chocolate bomb**

Delighted that the ticket is booked and that he is DEFINITELY coming over. Sex at last!! Nat, I'm going to leave you both to bond and not get dressed on Saturday night and see you on Sunday. You can both come over to mine before the others, so I get to see Ali on his own. Even if my trip to see Smurf is cancelled, I feel that you two should have that time on your own – first night and all that!

**February 18, 2000
From: Nic
To: Natalie
Re: Love potion – from Monsieur Gorgonzola**

*Finally opened it, how lovely! Hope the day wasn't too bad, know the feeling only too well, an early night for you tonight my girl!
Lots and lots of luck for the interview tomorrow, not that you need it and hopefully you will have had a damn good rogering by the time I see you on Sunday night.*

**February 18, 2000
From: Natalie
To: Nic, Andi
Re: Cheese**

Girls, why do I do it to myself! Still drunk, due to see you in a few mins and not sure how I am meant to get through day ….

February 18, 2000
From: Andi
To: Natalie
Subj: Smelly rotten cheese

This sounds as shit as you looked this morning. Have a long bath, mud pack on face and make yourself look and feel beautiful for the ARRIVAL tomorrow. Loads of luck for the interview, and enjoy, enjoy enjoy the big hugs of Ali.
Speak to you at some point tomorrow – will you book Café Med?
Love ya loads,
Andi

February 21, 2000
From: Natalie
To: Nic, Andi
Re: Monsieur Gorgonzola is on holiday!

Dearest both,
As you may be aware, Monsieur Gorgonzola is going to be off the net for the next week. Sorry to bail out on the daily cheese, please send me any which may wing its way between you two or any other mail the Monsieur Gorgonzola may appreciate.
I think Ali got the measure of the true beauty of our relationship last night, seemed to think we all had something very special. OK. Loved up and time to nip back to bed in attempt to suggest to Ali that perhaps we should get up. Shame it's so pissy, but hey, Monday and what a great day to be leaving London.
McD, special back rub for you – take it easy and Kissman, get your ass down here for Friday night.
Love,
Nat

February 28, 2000
From: Natalie
To: Nic, Andi
Re: warm cheesy scone with melted cheese

Dearest girls,

I hope that is a sufficient amount of cheese for you, but basically, I hope you get the picture. I am cheesed up, literally after the amount I have eaten of it this week, but also because I am blissfully happy and have a big grin on my face. OK, so the man has gone, for the while, but I can simply think of some thing and the grin appears.

So, well and truly lurved up and even this hour on a Monday morning can't dent my feeling of happiness. By tonight, I may be feeling a little different after the expected barrage from the beloved kids.

Now have confirmed offer of a job in Istanbul, all the paperwork will be coming in the next 3-6 weeks. I am going to be buggered if it limits my travel opportunities. Hmm, beginning to fancy it, I must say. Long time off and no decision to be made now. I must dash, will be out of touch until Wednesday night as have to prepare for the training day, all phone calls welcome. Anyone for soup and wine mid-week, ER, luuvy, gushy … gossip?

Love you both, small birds singing around my head, tulips …

Nat

February 28, 2000
From: Nic
To: Andi, Natalie
Re: Tickets for Private view at the Tate

Girls,

I have tickets for a private view at the Tate on Monday, March 27. Ruskin, Turner and the Pre-Raphaelites. I'm going to go to get my monthly culture fix, fancy joining me and then doing what we do best and have dinner? Let me know!

Nic

February 28, 2000
From: Andi
To: Nic, Natalie
Re: Tickets for private view

I'd love to, but that's the week I'm away on holiday in New York and seeing Flo.
Sorry, but you'll have to be culture buffs without me.
By the way, registered at the doc surgery on Cranwich. Great surgery, so Nic get
your arse down there and register.
Maybe a veg session on Friday if I'm not toooo peopled out! Actually I'm never
too peopled out for you two.
Love and snogs,
McD

February 29, 2000
From: Natalie
To: Nic, Andi
Re: Crumpets with lashings of salted butter and cheddar

Dearest girls,
As you can see, the taste buds are flowing even at this early hour. Nothing can
dampen the feel-good thing, still floating around, someone had better come
and drag me off the ceiling pretty soon or I may never come down. Spent last
night pouring over a map of Istanbul, the school is on the southern tip, next to
the sea of Marmara, (good earthquake territory!) Needless to say, did not do
very much work, then floated off to bed after too many cigs, coffees, wine …
ate my chocolate game (whoops, what a pig I am!)

Nic, Cate B would love to do the dinner thing tomorrow night. She is staying at
mine tonight, but not home til late, it's her first film session tonight!
Good going, girls – love you loads and Andi, hope you are up and running.
In for chats tonight, if anyone needs to hear my dulcet tones.

March 2000

January 4, 2000
From: Natalie
To: Andi
Subject : Welcome home

Dearest girls,
The sun is shining, it's Wednesday morning and today is a training day. No noise of the little loves yelling abuse, instead simply the tweeting of teachers in Cannonbury. I have to do a slot, but it is prepared, and I am looking forward to it. "Active approaches to Sex Ed" – the mind boggles, no thank you, we will not be having a floor show!
Still blissfully happy, but seem to have got myself into one of those tricky situations, drinks with Cairn. I am big enough to deal with it, so meeting in Mash tomorrow at 8 for anyone who would like to witness it all.
Really looking forward to a soup concoction at Nic's tonight, will bring blender, anything else you need, just mail! Andi, is it tonight you are out with your friend or tomorrow? Either way you will be missed, can we girls do Friday? I totally forgot but Jac and Simon arrive on Saturday. I will probably cook big boozy dinner for anyone interested. It sounds like they have had a wonderful time. Now on their way to NY where Simon will start a job.
Girls, love you loads, tips on how to behave on Thursday without giving wrong message, Ali is the only one for me. Pretty bloody cheesy!
Love,
Nat

March 2, 2000
From: Natalie
To: Nic, Andi
Re: Stilton Souffle

Dearest girls,

First, thanks Nic for wonderful night. I really enjoyed myself, at times a little too damned hot and heavy for my liking, but remember not to believe every thing you hear.

Now, re date, feeling icky, not into it, uncomfortable. Silly me will have to extract myself elegantly from this situation. Or the scarier alternative is get blind drunk and irresponsible which is not an option. I feel that I simply do not want other man in any capacity, so will have to let Cairn know - in a nice fashion, or Clairol as sister Lucy likes to call him.

Need to dash and make lunch, see you Friday, I hope. Could do with seeing just the 2 of you.

Love,

Nat

March 2, 2000
From: Andi
To: Nic, Natalie
Re: Tuna and cheese toasted melt

Morning! Just about to jump into a bath full of beautiful Floris smells and bubbles as well (ooh, how I spoil myself) and then off to the last day of the show. It's gone well so far and in fact I've really enjoyed being out of the office and with my client - a true salesperson. Tonight is the night with my special friend. Drinks, followed by Tango Dos at Sadlers Wells and then a spot of dinner. How lurvely! Nat, I reckon for the arm's length approach tonight, you need to babble on endlessly about your wonderful week with a very special man you met in Turkey - the problem is, that knowing men, that will just make him come running. Sod's law! Nic, how did Monday morning go at work - need to hear everything. I've missed you both and can't wait to see you tomorrow or Saturday. Off to my bath.

March 2, 2000
From: Natalie
To: Andi
Re: Wonderful night?

Dearest McD,

Hope you have a wonderful night tonight. I really couldn't face the prospect of being out with a man, if it's not Ali, I have it pretty bad. So, I pleaded illness, I didn't want to have to play some silly game. Have had a wonderful night snoozing in front of the telly and am about to have candlelit bath with bomb. Hope you are on for tomorrow night, will send usual morning mail and catch up with you after work.

Lots of love,

Love-sick friend

March 3, 2000
From: Natalie
To: Nic, Andi
Re: Croque Madame

Dearest girls,

Too damned wet to be bloody chirpy. In fact, feeling very relaxed and mellow, instead of doing the date thing last night, I said I was ill, disconnected the phone, had a scented bath with smelly candles and read a wonderful travel book about you know where. Simply could not face man, if it's not Ali. I am not interested plus feeling peopled out. Blanche still here and Jac and Simon arriving tomorrow. Hope you are both around tonight – perhaps chez McD? So, final day of week, hope you had wonderfully romantic night, Andi. A lot to chat about later.

Love,

Nat

Classic lemon cheesecake

You will need:

100 g digestive biscuits
40 g butter
250 g cream cheese
280 ml double cream
100 g caster sugar
Zest of 2½ lemons
5 tsp lemon juice
 (just under 2 lemons)
75 ml double cream

1. Line the base of an 18cm round loose bottomed tin with greaseproof. Melt the butter. Crush the digestive biscuits and add to the melted butter.

2. Put the biscuit mix into the prepared tin and use the back of a spoon to push it flat. Put the tin into the fridge to chill while you make the topping.

3. Finely grate the zest of 2½ lemons. Squeeze out the juice until you have enough for 5 tsp and set aside.

4. Whip the double cream until it forms a soft peak. Add the cream cheese, caster sugar, lemon zest and lemon juice. Whisk together until combined and thick.

5. Remove the tin from the fridge and add the lemon mixture. Add a little at a time and push the mixture down with the back of a spoon, so there are no gaps.

6. Once you've added all of your lemon mixture, smooth the top with a palette knife.

7. Put the cheesecake into the fridge for at least 2 hours to set fully.

8. When you're ready to serve, carefully remove the cheesecake from the tin. Whip the double cream until it forms stiff peaks and smooth over the top of the cheesecake. Zest a lemon and sprinkle over the top.

March 3, 2000
From: Andi
To: Natalie, Nic
Re: Mine it is

Mine it is … can't wait to see you both. Soup is readily available – a choice of butternut squash or … yep … you guessed it …PEA! However, more than happy to russle up pasta and salad if some one can buy some ingredients – sorry, guys, but I have sweet FA in the flat apart from the pasta part. Had a gorgeous evening last night. See you later for catch up. I'll probably be home by 7/7.30.
Love,
Andi XX

March, 6, 2000
From: Natalie
To: Nic, Andi
Re: Feta and raspberry jam pancake

Dearest grills,
Am I right or wrong in thinking that tomorrow is pancake day? In which case, doesn't anyone know how to make a bloody pancake without it becoming gooey sludge on the bottom of the pan? Thought the old salt and savory could be a winner! Well, in the words of the one and only Carol King "It's time to face another day" and I really could so easily do without, dragging feet and wishing the weeks away, a silly thing to do, I know. Hope that you two have a fabby dooby week if I don't see you, but in best cheese fashion, I know I will probably speak to you both every day and get all the gossip, follow up, especially from you, Nic. So, Monday beckons, I had better deal with it.
Love,
Nat

March 6, 2000
From: Nic
To: Natalie
Re: Feta and raspberry

Monday morning from hell with the boiler blowing out and cold bath, urghh! Slowly beginning to warm up, ready to face the day. Will catch up with you later, brrrr, lol.

March 6, 2000
From: Andi
To: Nic, Natalie
Re: Lemon and sugar pancake

I'm trying very very hard to wrangle a private pancake flipping lesson with the best chef in town! No guarantees that he'll be able to make it (his conscience sometimes get the better of him, much to my body's detriment!) but will let you know. Can I be really girlie and, if he lets me down, join my girlies for some pancakes with lemon and sugar?

March 6, 2000
From: Nat
To: Andi, Nic

Dearest McD,
Pleased to see that even in your busy and hectic life you have time for amusing mail. Spoke to Tom, give him a ring ce soir re Wednesday. It may be just Brad and I tomorrow for bonding, as Nic may have some bonding of her own to do, don't know if she is quite at the bondage stakes yet! Perhaps chat later, I will be in tonight doing sofa, telly, peace and waiting for call from man in Turkey.
Love,
Nat
PS – Nic, go for it and give him hell, as I know you will!

March 7, 2000
From: Andi
To: Nic, Natalie
Re: Pancakes with ricotta and honey

Nat, not sure if this means that you are home tonight or not? Fancy pancakes over at mine, let me know and I'll stop off on the way home and get the ingredients. I've got the late lunch option with my pancake flipper today, so no raunch tonight unfortunately! Delighted about the flat. I hope he sees it through this time and doesn't jerk about! I'm sure it's nice to have a clear idea in your mind as to what's happening, when etc. Nic, call me when you get home from seeing Richard, my favorite man!)
Catch you both later,
Andi XX

March 7, 2000
From: Natalie
To: Andi, Nic
Re: Pancakes with ricotta and honey

Dearest girls.

Am I right in thinking today is Pancake Day? I am really not sure of my dates, usually they have loads of Jiff lemon ads on telly and I haven't seen one. That aside, pancakes sound wonderful. Have arranged to have much needed drink with Penny after work. She won't need it, but I will. You know I am taking 20 students off to the theatre today, on the tube, through the West End, it should resemble a comedy sketch at the very least and quite possibly one of the less plausible disaster movies of recent years. Let's keep our fingers crossed that this will not become utter chaos, but where those kids are concerned, who the hell knows what will happen next/ Sorry, Nic, about the fruit, some way or another I will get it to you ce soir. Leave message of best way! Good news is that my buyer is back from NZ and so the deal is back on. This is just what the doctor ordered to stave off winter blues, so girls, will I hope soon be officially homeless. Good job you both have comfy floors and sofas. Also met fab Australian girl last night, friends of the travellers, she would be on for 29-pound Saturday night extravaganza in Paris, I think we should do it soon. A night to remember and a little decadent product buying on the way. For now, must prepare myself for the day ahead and take Jac and Simon to the bus stop – off to Victoria and Oxford.

Love,

Nat

March 8, 2000
From: Natalie
To: Nic, Andi
Re: Spaghetti carbonara (very cheesy sauce)

Dearest girls,

Was feeling very anti-social last night. It was such a joy having the flat to myself and wallowing on the sofa. In fact, was in bed asleep at 9.30 – oh what a late night I had. Foolish man, Cairn (?) rang again. I told him I was too busy and would call him when it suited me. That will teach me to get drunk and behave badly. Or not.

Yesterday's theatre trip was pretty uneventful, stolen ice creams from the bar, ashtrays, smoking on the street, heckling the actors, all seemed fairly tame for our kids. Some of them even enjoyed the play and listened. Wow. Well, tonight I have the horrid psycho babble birds in to do staff therapy, so you can imagine the mood I will be in. Fortunately having dinner with parentals tonight and so will take it out on a hot curry.

Nic, will call you and appear, perhaps in time for ER with your fruit! Or leave it on the step.

OK, sweets, love ya loads, really looking forward to weekend away – food, pampering, shopping … how bloody wonderful!

Nat

XX

March 8, 2000
From: Nic
To: Natalie, Andi
Re: Spag carbonara in very cheesy sauce

All are most welcome over at mine. I fancy a treat, so will be buying some fresh double cream for an amaretto/Tia Maria coffee, any takers?

Speak with you both later.

March 8, 2000
From: Andi
To: Nic, Natalie

Hello dearests,

I think we were all a little anti-social last night and just wanted peace and quiet on our respective sofas. I watched the most depressing documentary on Lene Zavaroni and went to bed feeling lucky to have a sane mind, a love for food and a happy, content life. Also, can't wait for the weekend. Mike and Hannah (his fiancé) may also meet up with us as they will be in Bristol for the weekend. It would be great to see them. I reckon I'll be home in time for ER, so I shall call and see who's around for a coffee.

Catch you later.

Love,

Andi

March 9, 2000
From: Andi
To: Nic, Natalie
Re: Pizza with loads a cheese

Had a shit night last night as my car got broken into and my laptop computer stolen! Will tell all when I see you both. Should be home by approx. 9pm tonight so will call when I get home. In need of a hug.

A XXXXX

March 9, 2000
From: Natalie
To: Andi, Nic
Re: Pizza with loads a cheese

Dearest girls. It is Thursday, and I for one am celebrating that fact. Almost feels like the beginning of the weekend and what a weekend it will be. I will be in tonight, so let's chat about where and when to meet tomorrow, also could do with lift to Islington and chuck bag into back of car. Keep it short, flat going on, survey being done on Friday. Think will have Blanchett chick here tonight. Well, looking forward to some quality time with you guys.

Love,

Nat

XX

March 12, 2000
From: Andi
To: Nic, Natalie
Re: Lurvely weekend

Nearests and dearests … what a fabby dabby weekend, full of all the things a girl would want (well nearly!) I wish we were wealthy enough to go somewhere new every weekend and indulge … perhaps in another life that's what we are doing, which is why I feel so comfortable lounging in beautiful hotel rooms and eating divine food. I wonder ….

Anyway, another week is about to commence and who knows what little delights will be instore. Keep me informed of any excitement and see you no doubt very soon.

Love always,

A

March 13, 2000
From: Nic
To: Andi, Natalie
Re: Smoked binkle with cream cheese

Ever the adventurer Andi, look forward to the three-way thing later! Having very busy day both with work and working out the love life. As far as I'm concerned, stay obsessed. It's great!!!!!

Speak to you both later.

March 13, 2000
From: Andi
To: Nic, Natalie
Re: Smoked binkle with cream cheese.

Kissman, tell me more … I'm intrigued. I'm in tonight as I've not heard a dickie bird from Cate and co about meeting up, so will speak to you both later – maybe we can try the 3-way thing on the phone. That sounds as sexual as smoked binkle. I'm getting obsessed – HELP! I need sex and will ravish poor Big as soon as he walks through the door. Hope you're still online Nat and get this.

Tiramisu
(with ricotta cheese)

You will need:

500g ricotta
250g Greek yogurt
80g caster sugar
2tsp vanilla extract
200ml cold strong coffee
1tsp ground cinnamon
24 savoiardi (sponge finger biscuits)
Cocoa powder, for dusting

1. Mix the ricotta cheese with the yogurt and sugar in a large bowl. Add the vanilla extract and stir until well combined.

2. Pour the cold coffee into a small bowl and mix in the cinnamon.

3. Quickly dip half the sponge fingers in the coffee and then place in the base of a rectangular serving dish (30 x 22cm and at least 5cm deep).

4. Spread half of the ricotta mixture on top. Repeat the process with the rest of the ingredients.

5. Cover the dish with clingfilm and leave to rest in the fridge for 15 minutes. Just before serving, dust the top with the cocoa powder.

March 13, 2000
From: Natalie
To: Andi, Nic
Re: Cheesecake with warm butterscotch sauce and banana

Dearest girls,

It was a truly wonderful weekend full of all the best of everything, almost, just one obvious thing missing. We laughed, we drank too much, we definitely ate too much, we shopped and snoozed our way through the weekend. After it all, I fell into bed at about 9.30 last night and was promptly to sleep. Wonderful, had flat to myself! Woke up feeling decidedly fat and determined not to go down that road, hmmm, struggle to eat healthily when faced with all those nummy things to eat. Will get back on track this week so any visitors to the kitchen chez moi will discover soups and salads and fruits, ok. Enjoy the first day back, hope all is well with the world of work – I only have 6 weeks to go.
Natalie

March 13, 2000
From: Andi
To: Natalie, Nic
Re: Cheesecake with warm butterscotch sauce and banana

Don't rub it in, Portman… we don't want a weekly reminder as to how few weeks you have left in the corporate arena – OK!! Did you manage to catch up with Tom? I'll try and ring him tonight and see when he's free. Sorry that I'm missing out on tomorrow night's bonding, but I have my own bond-ing .. age to do!
Love ya both,
Andi

March 14, 2000
From: Andi
To: Natalie, Nic
Re: Smoked binkle on muffin with lashings of hollandaise

Let's just say that if you do see me & Big later, it's because the stockings haven't worked. Here's hoping that my binkle is truly smoking later!!! Oh Miss MdD, you are a one! Catch you both tomorrow – Kissman, are you at Liverpool Street or do you need a lift tomorrow?
Sloppy kisses,
Andi

March 14, 2000
From: Nic
To: Andi, Natalie

How do you do it every morning? Was mine and Andi's question in the car, but God love ya for it, really sets me up in a good mood for the rest of the day and what, may I ask, is wrong with the binkle!! Andi looking v sexy this morning! Lucky Big, don't think coffee will be a thought tonight, other things on their minds! Looking forward to seeing you tonight, will give you a ring when I get in.

March 14, 2000
From: Natalie
To: Nic, Andi

Dearest girls,
The binkle theme could run and run. Gets the mind going in the morning and keeps the mind well and truly below pant level. Had lovely evening which included giggling to very amusing re-run of 'Have I got news for you', reading Rough Guide to Turkey and wondering whether I can travel into Syria from said country. No croaky Turk on phone, too busy drilling precious stones no doubt! Am really looking forward to catering for Nic and Hunter P. Will cook healthy and balanced dinner, don't' worry. You will be spared the delights of bean soup. Perhaps filo parcels and salad, set good example for Brad. Andi, what a shame you can't be with us and Big. Well, if neither of you can perform then rock by for coffee, or even better, perform and then rock by for coffee. So, on that binkle tingling thought (Our mails are becoming a little crude) have fab Tuesday … oh what do I have in store today? Trip to farm over road. Love happy clappy friend – do you think sandal-wearing is advisable in March?

March 15, 2000
From: Andi
To: Natalie

It's wonderful to hear you are so excited and lurved up – I fully agree that you're a dunderhead, but have tried to keep that to myself over the last month! Just go over and share the great news with him – the enjoyment you are feeling at the moment will be doubled by sharing it with him. They say that "a problem shared is a problem halved" well …….McD says a delight shared is a delight doubled! Book a flight and go, for God's sake. You have nothing to lose and everything to gain. You must remember that, generally speaking, people don't think in the same way as you, and I'm sure Ali in particular will be able to live off the anticipation of you spending some serious time in Istanbul.
Ok, enough of the McD ramble, just go and bloody well sort yourself out.
Love,
Andi

March 15, 2000
From: Natalie
To: Nic, Andi
Re: Seared binkle with wasabi dressing

Dearest girls,
You may want to cross your legs for binkle of the day! Had top night made all the better by appearance from Ms McD, hot from the bed of luurve. So, talk of the devil, the beloved Ali man rang last night. He is so bloody lovely, he told me to check my mail and he has sent me really moochy mail, could he really be in love? I really do want to tell him about the whole Istanbul thing and was almost going to spill last night, if Cate B hadn't arrived at the crucial moment in the conversation. I am thinking of going over for weekend or something, because if not it will have to wait til May which is a long way off and that is when I rock up with bag set for my travels round Turkey. I am a dunderhead. So like my mother, we think everyone is going to react to the things in the way we would react. Had brief chat with Blanchett chick last night, good so will be seeing her for late lunch and bottle of wine on Thursday after school. What it is to be a bloody part-timer. Have fab night Andi with Brad and Joel. Good one, Nic.
Love,
Nat

March 16, 2000
From: Nic
To: Natalie
Re: Binkle dipped in milk chocolate with a dusting of cocoa

For one horrible moment, I thought you were home already!!! Well, horrible for me, wonderful for you! Thanks for the pep talk, just need to have a winge every so often, as you say. Roll on the weekend and the alcohol fuzz.

March 16, 2000
From: Natalie at unix
To: Nic

Dearest,
I am doing something new and naughty, I am mailing you from work, fantastic. Don't feel stressed by the dilemmas which life throws at you. See it as a way of keeping you asking yourself questions which we hope will ultimately lead to greater satisfaction and fulfilment in our lives. What a load of psycho babble shit – load of crap. It's shite feeling like that, and I know where you are coming from. The only cure is good friends and bottle of wine. Roll on the w/end. Love, Nat

March 16, 2000
From: Natalie
To: Nic, Andi

Hope all had fab night last night. Brad rocked in last night to find me on sofa in state of exhaustion. Missed part 1 of ER, but part 2 was damned good. Had wonderful night myself at Forest Gate. Was welcomed by the students with open arms, Ben (deputy head) virtually snogged me and Andy (the head) said when you are back from Istanbul, let me know. I felt wonderful, certainly swelled the ego! Girls, you are so wise, I agree, Andi, I should nip over to Istanbul to tell Ali. I may do that once the Americans have been in a few weeks' time. He sent me wonderful, loving mail this morning, I said I would be out there in spring, and his response was "This will be a gift for me to have you here." So, girls, I for one am looking forward to movie on Saturday, what about early evening movie in London's finest west end followed by a few drinks in some good bar? We could pretend to be the beautiful people. Nic, you are not the only one who gets to do great lunches. Cate B and I are doing the cheap- skates version of it, Pizza Express, Islington at 4.30 for late lunch and bottle of wine, so girls, I will have a nice day. Enjoy your evenings!

Spag Carbonara
with very cheesy sauce

You will need:

400g spaghetti
1 tbsp olive oil
200g smoked pancetta cubes
  or streaky bacon, chopped
2 garlic cloves, crushed
3 eggs
75ml double cream
100g Grana padano or parmesan,
  finely grated, plus extra to serve

1. Bring a large, deep pan of salted water to the boil. Place spaghetti in the water, stir well and cook, following pack instructions. Aim for 'al dente': cooked, but retaining some bite in the middle.

2. Heat the olive oil in a frying pan. Tip in the pancetta. Fry over a medium heat until the fat in the meat has melted down into the pan and the meat has turned lightly golden. Remove from the heat and set aside.

3. Crack two of the eggs into a mixing bowl. Add the yolk from the third egg and beat together, along with the double cream, parmesan and some seasoning.

4. Add the garlic to the pancetta and return the frying pan to hob. Fry over high heat for 1 min or until garlic is cooked and pancetta warmed through. Drain the spaghetti. Tip back into the hot saucepan off the heat. Pour egg mixture over pasta, followed by hot pancetta, garlic, any fat and oils. Toss quickly and thoroughly with spaghetti spoon or tongs. Mix until it has thickened to a smooth, creamy sauce. Serve with extra cheese and freshly ground pepper.

March 16, 2000
From: Andi
To: Natalie
Re: Need a damn good shag

WILL THIS DO AS A SYMBOL? (Editor's note – obscene and unprintable!)

March 16, 2000
From: Natalie
To: Andi

Dearest McD, as have just said to Nic, am doing this at work. Don't know how but got rid of all the kids this afternoon and enjoying having no one looking over me. Fab, so please you liked the attachment, I haven't really looked at it, but is there a symbol for "need a damned good shag"? Let me know if you find it. Cinema fab, good movies being released. Will get Guardian guide on Saturday.
Love,
Nat

March 17, 2000
From: Natalie
To: Nic
Re: Showsavers – Carmen offer

Dearest,
Sorry about pains, once more at work mailing, about to go home! Yes for tomorrow, let's do Mark 1, while we are at it. Do you think she means March/April? I said why don't I pay using vouchers, sounds good to me.
Chat tomorrow.
Love,
Nat

March 17, 2000
From: Natalie
To: Nic, Andi
Re: Café latte at Starbucks

Am off for damned good coffee before work, feeling the strain of dragging myself out of bed for a job I have no commitment to. Also feeling a bit grey, today, or is it blue, not sure why but just am. Spoke to Tom last night, he is on for movie on Saturday night, I have time out and there are endless choices we could go for, just really depends on which area we want to go to the cinema in. Let me know if you have any movie preferences, I thought perhaps we could go to Curzon Soho, or Mayfair depending what they have on and then bottle of wine afterwards. Tonight, having dins with parents, will be up and on for market tomorrow morning, if anyone else fancies. So, let's chat tonight. Shared bottle of wine with Blanchett chick yesterday after work, she seems fine, has taken cash job couriering around London. Looking forward to a dose of the girls this weekend!
Love,
Nat

March 17, 2000
From: Andi
To: Nic, Natalie
Re: Quality weekend

What about 'The Talented Mr Ripley'? I'll check out where it's on in the West End. Also, the film that Michael Cain is in is getting some good reviews. Will speak to you later, as I'm over at Mum's tonight. I'd love to do the market with you tomorrow, but 9am sounds a bit early me. A lie-in on a Saturday morning is essential to the well being of one's soul … me thinks!
Love ya,
Andi

March 17, 2000
From: Andi
To: Nic, Natalie
Re: Quality weekend

Just spoke to Nat and we will probably go later to the market at approx. 11am, so I think we'll have to buy our avocados separately.

March 19, 2000
From: Andi
To: Natalie, Nic
Re: Discount flights

My new email address with freeserve … now I have a choice … oo-er Mrs.!
I woke early this morning and seem to have spent the last couple of hours surfing. Such fun. I now know who's playing at which jazz bars when we're in NYC, which is the best play in town and what ludicrous fares they charge for a flight down to Raleigh Durham. Anyway, regardless of how difficult my search is, though you would like to have a play around with these 3 sites :-
www.travelocity.com
www.air-far.com/lowest
www.airlinereservations.net
Downstairs are humping like rabbits – she's got some serious staying power, as she's been moaning and shouting "yes, yes" for the last 1.5 hours and she's still going!!
Nat, speak to you later.
Big kiss,
A

March 20, 2000
From: Natalie
To: Nic, Andi
Re: Double choc chip chocolate brownie

Had real difficulty dragging myself out of the bed this morning, perhaps too much sleep as I was tucked up and light out by 10. Am I slipping into middle age so soon, or just learning to enjoy the delights and benefits of sleep.
So, Monday again. I only have 4 to go, including this one, that's a pretty wonderful thought. Tonight, I imagine it will be shop-bought quiche and house salad, bottle and coffee. All welcome, just mail and let me know. Nic, I am looking forward to hearing about the personal trainer and how the whole thing works. OK, sweets, see you tonight, hope you can make it, Andi.
Love,
Nat

March 20, 2000
From: Nic
To: Natalie

How lovely to see your happy face in the car behind us this morning. I'm amazed how it can happen, of all the cars in all the world etc! Will bring bottle opened last night around as only half glass drunk and will probably need it after my first session, the thought of parting with all that money!
Hope you had a good day. Catch you later.

March 20, 2000
From: Andi
To: Nic, Natalie
Subj: Real men DO eat quiche!

Dearest both,
I believe that with middle age comes an appreciation for the finer things in life- sleep included. So, I guess that means – no, I correct myself, we're all still spring chickens and middle age is still a lifetime away!
See you both tonight – just the 3 of us.

March 21, 2000
From: Natalie
To: Nic, Andi
Re: Do real men eat baked goat's cheese flan?

Dearest girls,
What a fab night last night. How we laughed, I am simply so disappointed in the managing director. For some reason leapt out of bed full of beans at 6 this morning, thought it was sunny, it was so bright until realized it was seasonal dose of London fog. So, thinking of the date thing last night, and happening to have time out next to my bed last night, I think I have found the ultimate professional "I am not looking for a date" dating agency. It also fulfils certain things which Kissman has often discussed before, so see following:
EuroClub
Living or working in London area?
Want to improve on your European language?
Non-profit club offers social events and inexpensive tuition ......
http://www.euroclub.co.uk
Girls, I think this is a great way to improve language and also meet Italian, French, Czech ... men. If English ones just can't cut the mustard, go further afield.
So, on that note, starving this morning, think I will stop at Starbucks for Grande skinny hot choc before work. Really must do some work today as have loads of reports to be done tomorrow! Whoops, forgot all about it, oh well. Have coffee date with Azad today, should be fun?
Love,
Chirpy Nat

March 21, 2000
From: Andi
To: Nic, Natalie

Delighted you're so chirpy. I was in the most stinking mood this morning and the pump not working at the petrol stations made things 10 times worse. Still grumpy, but hoping that the day will get better. Will chat later.
Snogs,
McD

March 22, 2000
From: Nic
To: Natalie, Andi
Re: Sticky risotto with molton cheese, bubbling

Darling girls,
Very interesting course on PB and the business in general, lovely not to be at my desk, but still in the building, hence able to email! Going for a drink with Nigel tonight, but rarely is it a late one so may well rock up at yours for the ER Sex/City sess!!! Altho probably a bit worse for wear!!!
Catch you later, you too Andi, I hope.

March 22, 2000
From: Natalie
To: Nic, Andi

Dearest girls,
Had fab dinner last night, the remnants of our dinner the other night, much better reheated. A little merry by 6.30 last night, into second glass, peaked at 8, in bed by 9, asleep with sequel to Bridget Jones by 10, wide a-bloody-wake by 3! That will teach me to go to bed so damned early. Do any of you wish to entertain me during ER and Sex in the City, ok Andi, so you may just have had some sex in the city of your own, but the rest of us have to get our kicks where we can. A dull and bitty day ahead, so trying to get there early. Enjoy, I have feeling that Kissman is on course and will not get this til Friday, and of course I know where McD is. Andi, give Myrt a ring.

March 24, 2000
From: Nic

To: Natalie
Re: Toasted cheese, peanut butter and tom sarnie

Sounds good to me, will ring when I get up.

March 24, 2000
From: Natalie
To: Andi, Nic

Dearest girls,

Slept like babe on sofa. Feel gorgeous in comparison to yesterday's horror. Running late for me on Friday. So will keep this short and sweet. Really enjoyed ballet, next one is on me, have those blinking vouchers. Will discuss dates and what at the w/end. Andi, see ya at Myrts. Nic, fancy market/spec savers tomorrow? Give me ring when you wake up. TGIF.

Love,

Nat

March 26, 2000
From: Andi
To: Nic, Natalie
Subj: See you in a week

Girlies,

What a fab Sunday. Thanks, Nic, for playing hostess with the mostest. I'll miss the ol' cheesy mail this week and will try and send one from North Carolina, just so I can be part of the goings on in Stamford Hill. You'll be glad to hear that anal McD has done her packing AND the flat looks like a million dollars … or at least 160 squids. I'm already dreaming of a new place with patio for drinks in the summer – I must calm myself down and just wait and see what happens. The bummer is that even if I do get my place for the summer, neither of you will be here to share it with me. Boo hoo hoo ⍰

Anyway, on a cheerier note, IM OFF TO NEW YORK!

Love you both and will see you in a week's time.

Big wet sloppy kiss

Andi

March 27, 2000
From: Nic
To: Natalie
Re: What, no cheesy mail!

Natalie P., the disappointment is acute! But the day saved by Andi's bon voyage note. Hope all is well, so unlike you, will call later. Just arrived at work, changed all my clocks I could, but forgot to change my mobile phone which doubles up as the alarm clock! Very bad and very late.

March 27, 2000
From: Natalie
To: Andi, Nic
Re: Cheddar cheese

Dearest girls,
It was an utterly perfect day as far as I was concerned, even down to the spaghetti carbonara. What a shocker this morning is, damned-grey, wet and dark, not a Monday to bother with, but I only have 2 more Mondays after today! Today's fun and games will consist of meeting with parent at 8.30, smear test this afternoon and then buyer coming round. So, a real laugh as you can probably tell. Really felt tired this morning and not wanting to spring out of the bed. Thinking of you, McD, up up and away today. Have a damned fantastic time. Speak to you, Kissman. Let's indulge ourselves with a Friday night of good booze in some of London's finest.

March 28, 2000
From: Natalie
To: Nic
Re: Pea soup?

Dearest Kisser,
Just you and me for the next week, but I think we will cope. So, in order to get through this trying time without McD, do you fancy a bottle of wine, a bowl of soup ce soir once you have been pushed and pulled at gym?
Let me know if it suits, I am sure I will be home at disgustingly early time this afternoon.
Hope all is fabby dooby, any news on where Mastrict is (is that even how it's spelt?)
OK sweets – later
I DID SEND MAIL!

March 29, 2000
From: Natalie
To: Nic
Re: Haddock and sweetcorn chowder

Dearest Nic,
Despite the fact that fell into bed after you had gone, Bridget kept me awake til late, so finally have broken the back of the stupid sleep pattern. It's really quite amusing and perfect for the lazy read without any brain cells actually being required to do anything.
Horrid morning, I wonder if you really did drag yourself into work for 7, oh me of little faith, or are you still tucked up in bed all cosy and warm. Will give you a tinkle tonight to see if you are up to amaretto coffee and ER session. Sounds damned good to me.
Oh, another joyful day at the chalk face begins, yippy can hardly wait. I may be bruised and battered wreck by the time I see you, once have told kids of imminent departure. On the Friday front, was thinking would suggest to Cate B we meet up in the West End, as I do want to come home on Friday night as have lots of flat things to do on Saturday, market, hair … think on if you can make it.
See you later – Nat.

April 2000

April 4, 2000
From: Natalie
To: Andi
Re: Welcome back!

Dearest McD,
I am really looking forward to seeing you guys tonight. I need a bit of gossip and light relief. I seem to spend all my time at the moment being cheerful and dashing between bits of my life, the hospital, Dad … it was fab that Cath came over, she is very good at organizing dad. Things are not actually very good in reality, Mum can't walk almost at all, she is very weak, in constant pain and depressed. Dad is stressed and panicking, but not actually doing anything very constructive. I do not know how they will manage at Eton Ave. They need help and have to sell the house. All pretty sad really. I just am counting the days until I can go away, one month, and then time for myself.
Really can't wait to see you tonight. Hopefully Nic will join us. She doesn't know what time she will be home, but if we are round the corner at Centurion, then she will meet us there. Will let myself into flat, 7.30 ish. Will go see Mum after work.
Love,
Nat

April 4, 2000
From: Andi
To: Natalie
Re: Welcome back

Sweet stuff,

I can't wait to see you either. I am so sorry to hear that things with your Mum are not looking too good – you sounded fairly positive yesterday on the phone. I'm sure I'll be out of work on time, so will see you at mine. No word from Brad as yet, so I hope he has a set of keys and can let himself in. Can't wait to see you.
Love,
Andi

April 4, 2000
From: Natalie
To: Andi, Nic
Re: Wonderful night

Dearest girls,

It was wonderful seeing you last night. Good to share bottle of wine, good food and general news. Hoping that no heating at work in which case will not stay long! Let's hope then I can have indulgent day reading papers …

Had message from Tom last night, am going to send him mail saying Brad is in town, so he may get in touch. I will drop by for coffee later. Hope you all have fab day, enjoy the family drive into work.

Love,

Natalie

PS Andi, can I have your Mum's phone number, want to ask her about removal men, do you have any suggestions?

April 4, 2000
From: Natalie
To: Andi
Re: Wonderful night

Dearest,

Thanks for mail. Am feeling shitty, achey, sore throat, not good. Will call later, but if feel shitty then will not come round. Off to see Mum. Think she will be in til end of week now. Dad chopped finger last night, so if I feel ok am going to do curry with him.

What a worry aged parents are!

Love,

Nat

April 4, 2000
From: Andi
To: Natalie
Subj: Hope you feel better

Where's this from? You poor thing – sounds shitty and the last thing you need. Just keep counting the days …. Hope to see you later for a warm mug of coffee.

Love,

McD

April 5, 2000
From: Natalie
To: Nic, Andi
Re: Sisters

Dearest girls,

Feeling bloody wonderful, bit under the weather, but has not developed into full scale flu thing. Can hardly wait, have lovely hospital appointment this afternoon, wonder what they will do to me! Will be in tonight on sofa, guys coming round to give me estimate of removal costs. Lucy, bless her heart, is coming over on Monday. I hope Mum and Dad will accept her presence gracefully. Anyway, it will be fab to see her.

Laters,

Nat

X

Butternut squash soup

You will need:

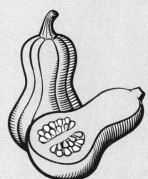

1.5kg peeled and deseeded butternut squash, cut into chunks
1 large onion, roughly chopped
2 medium carrots, peeled and chopped
4 tbsp olive oil
1 tbsp clear honey (optional)
1.5 litres vegetable stock
salt and freshly ground black pepper

1. Preheat the oven to 200C/180C Fan/Gas 6.

2. Tip the prepared squash into a large tray with the onion and carrots. Add the oil and salt and pepper and toss everything together until the vegetables are evenly coated.

3. Roast in the oven for 40–45 minutes, or until tender and tinged brown. Drizzle over the honey, if using, 5 minutes before the end of cooking.

4. Place the large, deep-sided saucepan over a medium heat. Pour in the stock and bring to the boil, then stir in the roasted vegetables and add salt and pepper.

5. Remove the saucepan from the heat and, using a hand blender, blend the mixture until smooth.

....

April 6, 2000
From: Natalie
To: Nic, Andi
Re: Glands

....

Dearest girls,

I am not at work today. Swollen glands, temp, weakness … rather enjoying it. Am going back to bed now. More later.

Love, Nat

....

April 6, 2000
From: Andi
To: Nic, Natalie
Re: Glands

....

What a shame we weren't both off together … my tummy is still feeling a little delicate, but no more vomit!!

Speak to you later.

Love, Andi

April 7, 2000
From: Natalie
To: Nic, Andi
Re: Are we all at work?

Dearest girls,

Typing fingers all feeling a little rusty. Am I right in thinking this will be our first day at work in 4 days (well, all of us at work)? I feel a whole lot better, still a little lumpy, but ok. Have to drag myself into work, as cooking pizza and ice cream for my tutor group. Plus, good news, think Mum is out of hospital today and have hot date tonight with Cath and Myrt, just to get in training for hen night tomorrow night. Am thinking tomorrow day will trek round London's finest West End, looking for cameras and email phones.

On the note of my travels, had wonderful chat with Ali. I broke the news that I would be traveling round Turkey, he was delighted and is already thinking about where and how often we can meet. Also seems that is he very keen I should meet his daughter. I was trying to squirm out of it, but guess I should bite the bullet. We will overlap for couple of days at the beginning of May. Hmmm, so interesting things afoot. All my paperwork has now arrived with the school. Have asked them to send it, but now think I should collect I when I am out there. There seems to be no obvious hurry, but will ask.

Speak later,

Love, Nat.

(Will be at Eton Ave most of the weekend)

April 10, 2000
From: Natalie
To: Nic, Andi
Re: Mayo and frites

Dearest girls,

I think our final mails need to move towards a more international flavour, in honour of Maastrict (?) I obviously thought of chips.

Just in case you had forgotten, today is my FINAL MONDAY FOR FOUR MONTHS – I am very sorry, but you know this is going to go on every day this week. Another wonderful night. Was chuckling to myself last night about us three. Chez moi ce soir pour all and sundry. There will be poulet salade, quand you get here. I hope I will be surrounded by bin bags of rubbish, piles of unwanted, but possibly lovely things for the two of you. This could be a little ambitious, perhaps I will simply get home and go straight to sleep.

Enjoy, enjoy – a plus tard,

Natttttt

April 10, 2000
From: Andi
To: Nic, Natalie
Re: Mayo and frites

Shit, I'm going to miss you two!! Talk about a routine and laugh at Big and I , but we have as much, if not more of a routine between the three of us. Sorry about that little sober note. I guess a bit of Mondayitus. Hope to see you for coffee later, after I'm canapeed out here at the hotel.

Can't wait to see my friend later – the sun is shining, so I think a sarnie and a cuddle in the park.

Love you both,

Andi

April 11, 2000
From: Natalie
To: Nic, Andi
Re: Belgium waffles with lashings of maple syrup

Dearest girls,

Hmm, thinking wonderful breakfast, glass of freshly squeezed juice, coffee, girls, gorgeous waiter. Instead have NOTHING in flat, no fruit, no real coffee, think this could be a Starbucky kind of morning (isn't every morning one of those for you two?) So, thought I would just remind you, it's the last TUESDAY at work for the next ... you know the form now. Really work is just a small inconvenience which is messing up the cleaning of the flat and getting on and doing what I need to be getting on and doing.

Hope you girls have a tippy top, fantastique, magnifique, ho-he-hon jour aujourd'hui.

Adieu pour maintenant – bises, bises,

Nattttt

XXXX

April 11, 2000
From: Nic
To: Andi, Natalie
Re: Belgium waffles

My head is swimming with financial talk which I won't bore you both with. More interesting things to find out like, did the earth move when you saw Big and is all fantastic with the world again, my darlin' Andi? Will need to catch up big time by end of the week and darling linguistic Natalie chilling out on how wonderful the world is about to become with what is it, the last Tuesday. Oh joy! I haven't confirmed a late drink evening with Chantal on Friday so can always rearrange if Nat can go ahead with tickets.

Love you both, leave you both and talk later. Back to corporate finance.

Nic

Pea soup

You will need:

1 tbsp olive oil
½ onion, chopped
200g frozen peas
300ml vegetable stock
50ml double cream
salt and freshly ground black pepper

1. Heat the oil in a saucepan over a medium heat. Add the onion and garlic and fry for 3–4 minutes, until softened.

2. Add the frozen peas and vegetable stock and bring to the boil. Reduce the heat and simmer for ten minutes.

3. Add the cream and use a hand blender to liquidise the soup.

4. Season, to taste

April 11, 2000
From: Andi
To: Nic, Natalie
Re: Belgium Waffles

You're a nutter you are (said without pronouncing the 't'). Indeed, had a banana and date muffin and a grande double shot latte – but no Nic – boo hoo. Not the same without you, love. How d'ya both fancy going to see the Brand New Heavies on Friday – something different je pense, as a little flit in London for the 3 of us. Let me know and I'll look into it.
Nat, hope you had a luuuuurvely evening with Lucia.
Andi
XX

April 11, 2000
From: Natalie
To: Andi
Re: Belgium waffles

Friday sounds fantastic! Where are BNH's playing? We could do that if it's not a huge venue okay eg Jazz Café style, if not then could alternative. So, comme il dit en France, have a bonne soiree. J'ai parle avec mes deux soeurs. Mum is back in, went in yesterday, having brain scan today, but we think she simply had a panic attack.
Speak soon.
Amber Moves are fab, moving next Wednesday, thanks to your sis.
Love y'loads,
Nat
XX

April 11, 2000
From: Andi
To: Natalie, Nic

They're playing at Brixton Academy - ok, so not local or a small venue, but what a giggle and such fab music. We could get the tube all the way there or drive. I would really LOVE to go, but need someone to be my friend and come too!!! Sympathy sometimes works, but somehow, I've never had great success with you, so I'll just beg.
How long are they expecting Una to be in hospital? What a pain for her to be back in - I think I'll wait to send the balloon in a box - can't imagine it going down too well in St. John's Wood. Delighted that you've sorted out a move date - get your arse in gear and start packing.
Love ya,
AM

April 11, 2000
From: Andi
To: Nic, Natalie
Subj: Earth Moving

The earth moved, baby, and yes, the insecurities of McD have been squashed like a rather annoying fly and the world is fantastic again.
Nic, we just need to convince Nat that it's worth schlepping to Brixton to see them play - either drive or tube all the way there. Come on, girls. Let's do it!

April 12, 2000
From: Natalie
To: Andi, Nic
Re: biftek et frites

Dearest girls,

The number of mails flying between you two it's any wonder you get any work done, says smug Portman and, guess what, LAST WEDNESDAY for four months! Today though may make up for all the working days I will be missing. It's Chessington World of Chaos day today, the weather is crappy, the kids are nuts and the teachers just want to get through the day so we can collapse in the pub. If you would like to pitch up for a drink, we will be in the bar in Canonbury. It's called something like 25 Canonbury. Drunken teachers may not be your scene.

It was grand seeing sister yesterday, she looks fab. Mum is still in hospital, not sure when she will be out. They are running tests for scary things, has the cancer spread to the brain, tumour, or perhaps nothing …

I am ecstatic, my contract arrived yesterday from the school. All looks fab to me, so have signed my life away. Boxes arrive on Saturday morning, so the process begins in earnest.

I think I will skip the BNH. It's not my scene and you forget I am about 164 sometimes. I will probably do flat stuff and catch up with big sister and the fam. Enjoy today at work, girls. Today will be a very long day!

Love,

Nat

April 12, 2000
From: Andi
To: Natalie
Subj: Friday night

Dearest,

Hope the hangover hasn't quite kicked in yet and that your last real drinking binge with work mates was fun.

Looks like the night out in Brixton isn't going to happen – I thought it might too much to get all 3 of us to want to go to South London – never mind.

Out with Big tomorrow night but hope to catch up with you and maybe Lucia over the weekend. What about dins on Friday? Just a thought, but I'm sure it depends on how your Mum is. Is there any news on the results of her tests and when she might be home?

Take care and enjoy your mug of tea and marmite on toast tomorrow morning – the café on Dunsmure is going to miss you!

Love,

Andi

April 13, 2000
From: Natalie
To: Nic, Andi
Re: Hangovers

Dearest Chicksters,

Hmmm, head is doing that pounding thing. The saving grace is that I knew when to leave. Did not want to take responsibility for Penny again. She was ratted when I left, holding hands with the Australian supply teacher. Last time it was the music teacher. She will get herself a not very nice reputation for drunkenness.

Had good day at Chessington. Kids were excellent, right up til one of them got done shoplifting! But that was all, much less than any of us expected.

So, hoping I may see you girls this morning, as my car is in Canonbury. You know the thing.

Have fabby dooby day, this is my last day with the kids, and they will be gone by lunchtime. Two days at work left, was given lovely box of chocs and cheque which will go towards the camera.

See ya sweets. Guess Nic is very busy as there has been no mail from her – hmmm, hint, hint, do you think you have a job to do or something.

Love,

Nat

April 14, 2000
From: Natalie
To: Nic, Andi
Re: Dins ce soir

Dearest girls,

This day has been a long time in coming, but it's here. My last day at work. Nearly cleared up and sorted. Just have to get to the bottom of the files and marking and copying schemes of work and then I think I am done.

Penny is taking me out for lunch, not often that we get to do things like that. Has been a very good few days. Mum is home and on very good form. I think they may have given her some happy pills, but not sure, she has more pills than the local drug dealer. She is up, thinking about getting on with things.

Big sis would love to meet Nic and of course catch up with Andi. If it's ok, let's do somewhere around Belsize Park. If you fancy, come round to Eton Ave for a glass of wine, Mum and Dad would love to see you both, have heard so many tales of you, Nic, and then we will go off for dins.

Hope you both had good, if not exhausting Thursdays. You sounded a little stretched, Nic, no complaints about not enough to do now, hey? And Andi was it out and drinking, or in and shagging? Feel like have lots to catch up on with you both.

Love, Nat

April 14, 2000
From: Nic
To: Andi, Natalie
Re: Final Day

Frantic, frantic, frantic!!!!! I will never say I am bored again, I know I lie! Andi, sounds like you had a fab time, can't wait for the gory details later/ Yes please for a lift, give us a ring when you are ready. Nat, you lucky lucky thing, last day!!! Plans for tonight sound great.

Love you both loads,

Nic

Feta and Raspberry Jam pancake

You will need:

4 eggs
340g flour
1 tsp baking powder
1 tsp salt
500 ml milk
6 tbsp oil
100g feta cheese
4 tbsp raspberry jam
Butter to serve

1. Mix together the sifted flour, salt and baking powder in a bowl. Separate the whites from the yolks.

2. Beat the whites to a fluffy snow, mix the beaten yolks with the milk, stir well.

3. Add the egg yolk mixture to the dry ingredients with a spatula while stirring. Add the beaten whites and stir slowly and carefully until the two mixtures combine into a fluffy batter. Add the crumbled feta cheese and mix it carefully with the mixture.

4. Heat a pan with a nonstick coating, smear it with a little butter, pour in 1/2 cup of the mixture and quickly spread it out along the bottom of the pan by shaking it.

5. Once bubbles start to form on the surface of the pancake, flip it over and fry briefly. Serve warm with butter melted on top and a spoonful of jam smeared over each pancake

April 14, 2000
From: Andi
To: Natalie, Nic
Subject: Final Day

It was shagging AND dinner – what a perfect combination. God, I love sex!! Tried to get into Centuria at approx. 9pm, but they were full, so tried the little Italian next to the bar you got pissed up in on Wednesday – delicious! Big on great form – wonderful evening all round. Really looking forward to seeing both and the Portman clan later. So pleased to hear that Una is up and feeling more chirpy. Nic, call me and we'll arrange a time to meet later. Nat – hope the last day was fun fun fun all the way. The final countdown has arrived.
Love, Andi

April 15, 2000

Dearest Sample,
Want to check that I have loaded my new address properly. Can you please respond to this email?
Thanks, Nat

April 15, 2000
From: Andi
To: Natalie
Subj: Is my new name - Sample?

Do I gather that I have changed my name and I am now called "Sample"? He he he ... guess you must have sent out a generic message to everybody – quite amusing the way it was addressed though.
Just set up my printer – it's fab and great quality print/ Managed to access the bank and print off statements. God, it's so clever what you can do from the privacy of your own home. You can picture it – me in my yellow dressing gown, mug of coffee on desk, BNH playing in the background AND meanwhile transferring money between accounts. SOOOOO COOOOOL! Anyway, just about to shower and make myself look half-way decent and then meet up with Kate for a spot of lunch. I might then mooch into town and checkout the Dickens & Jones sale and buy little Tom a birthday pressie for his first birthday.
Love, Andi
Nat – just tried to send and it's being rejected from the Hotmail address? Did you already leave without telling meeeee????

Afters

So, the 'Soup Diaries' finishes with Natalie headed off to live in Turkey with Ali, (not his real name), where she ran his hotel, made lots of friends, thought up all kinds of businesses that didn't work out, left the first Ali, started teaching English as a foreign language, became fluent in Turkish, founded her own school in Kumluca and married Ali 2, the love of her life.

Cancer plagued several of her later years, but that didn't slow her down one bit. She always said she had the best years of her life once she married the real Ali and she held tightly onto her quality of life with Ali and his daughter Suzy-Q (not her real name) until the very end. Sister died in the summer of 2018 and is buried next to Ali's father and other daughter, in the mountains overlooking the Mediterranean that she so adored.

Andi leaves Big and the big city, moves up North, and starts a baking business called 'Two Tarts.' There she meets the man who is to become her husband (an early customer of the Two Tarts market stall no less) and they build a beautiful life together in the Nottinghamshire countryside along with a series of doggies. Andi traveled back and forth to Turkey a lot to see Natalie and her lovely life; always meeting up in England too, when Natalie came back to see the family. Andi still works in the hotel industry and stays in touch with Natalie's family.

Nic moves to Brighton and commutes daily to London, still working in the world of banking and high finance. She meets her future husband and there begins a more civilized life of working less and loving more. She also traveled to Turkey many times before Natalie passed and they were firm friends to the end.

Cate bought a house in North London and had a beautiful baby with her partner. She still works in the film/TV industry and she also traveled back and forth to Turkey many times in the last years of Natalie's life, both alone and with her family. She and Natalie had been friends since they were very small children; nothing was going to alter that.

Email, texting, What's App, Facetime et al made sure that the girls were still and always in the room with one another, if only virtually. As was mentioned at one point in the story, 'now we can have virtual soup together every night!' And that is pretty much what happened. When the girls were all together, it was like they never left and that is what old friends are all about.

It has been both a privilege and an honor to compile this story for my baby sister and her friends. Thanks must go out to them for allowing me to take on the project, answer my questions, compile the recipes, and not boss me around too much. A huge thank you also goes to my old friend and epic graphic designer Lizzie for agreeing to design the 'Diaries' and paginate the piece. You saved me from the awful world of clip art and we are already collaborating on our next project about our childhood together on the East Coast of England.

And to all who think that some of the past is worth preserving, however small a piece. You're right.

Lots of love,
Big sis
Lu

ABOUT THE AUTHOR

Lucy Mason Jensen was born on the East Coast of England. She graduated from London University in 1986 and immigrated to the US in 1988 'for the fun of it'. She still lives there today on a rescue ranch in the Gabilan Range of California's Central Coast, surrounded by a multitude of babies of her heart – dogs, cats, chickens, horses, llamas, goats, a pig, turtles, birds and, most recently, cows and ducks all roam freely on the ranch. She also has three children and one granddaughter to date.

Lucy is the co-founder of South County Animal Rescue and the author of *Window on the World*, *Winston Comes Home*, *The Animals Teach Us Everything & Other Short Tails* and *The Rosebud & Her Brilliant Adventures*.

FROM THE DESIGNER

What a treat for my dearest old friend Lu to ask me to work on this delightful book with her... I've known Lucy (and her baby sis 'Nat') since I was about 4 years old (a very, very long time ago) and have since come to know the wonderful and dynamic women who feature in this endearing look-back to the heady days of youth in 90's London. The giddy (largely alcohol-laced!) conversations between these dear friends made me laugh so much, and are only slightly tinged by sadness at the fact that Nat is no longer with us, and that she left such a large hole in the lives of those who knew and loved her. By preserving this precious moment in time Lu, you have created not just a tribute to your amazing sister, but a powerful acknowledgement of the extraordinary strength of enduring friendships between women – 'Nat' was truly blessed to have such incredible friends.... as am I, to have you!

Lizzie